CATCHING
WITH UMBRELLAS

Rigging and Fishing in Saltwater and Freshwater

BY CAPT. STEVE TOMBS

PUBLISHER'S INFORMATION

EBookBakery Book

Author contact: shearwaterst@cox.net

ISBN 978-1-938517-60-0

1. Fishing. 2. Umbrella Rigs. 3. Saltwater. 4. Freshwater.
5. Conservation. 6. Bass Fishing

© 2016 by Stephen C. Tombs

TABLE OF CONTENTS

VI

ACKNOWLEDGMENTS

I have many people to thank for helping me pull this book together. First, I'd like to give a special thanks to Dan Vesuvio of Picasso Lures who was very helpful and willing to share some of his knowledge of fishing freshwater umbrellas and who provided several pictures and tips on Picasso's rigs. Troy Lehew and Shane Lehew of Shane's Baits also shared information on their castable umbrellas and Shane shared his FLW Tour bass experience using them. Many thanks to Joseph Oppager and the FLW photographers for sharing FLW's rules and some of their fabulous photos, as well as to Jason Schratwieser from the International Game Fish Association who helped clarify their stance on umbrella rigs.

A big thank you goes out to Stephen Sekora, son of the late great John Sekora (Captain John) of Montauk, New York fame. Stephen shared his knowledge about the history of the umbrella rig's development.

I want to thank Captain Joe Wysocki on several levels. First, he builds a great umbrella frame that I've used for years. I've literally caught thousands of fish with his frames. In addition, he shared some of his expertise on the subject to make this work better.

I also need to thank my high school English teacher, Ms. Corbiere. She would probably be mortified that out of all her students to have a book published, I was one of them. I guess I can say that I learned from at least some of those red comments that were proliferated throughout the margins of my papers (and on the backs of my papers, and on the additional pages attached). Thank you for attempting what might have seemed like a fruitless effort at the time.

Thank you to Susan M. Tombs for editing and for the moral support to undertake this work.

I'd like to thank Captain Alan Anderson for teaching me many things about fishing, about fish behavior, and about chartering. Al has been a good mentor in many ways in addition to being a friend. His legendary fishing record speaks for itself and his induction into the IGFA (International Game Fish Association) Hall of Fame was well deserved. I feel very fortunate to be able to have fished with him and know that I've probably only learned a fraction of what he has forgotten about this great sport.

A very special thank you to Michael Grossman who has helped me through the publishing process and guided me to the completion of this book. His knowledge and expertise was immensely helpful.

Last, but certainly in no way least, I would like to extend a very large thank you to my friends, family and customers who have fished with me throughout the years. You've met me at the dock at some ungodly hours, endured hours at a time of listening to bad jokes and country music, and supported my tag and release practices while still being able to wrestle a few fish away for dinner. I'm grateful for the time spent together on the water, and I enjoyed every minute of it (with a few notable exceptions of course!)

Dedication

I would like to dedicate this work to Robert Edward Tombs and Constance Anne Tombs who are otherwise known as "Mom and Dad". Whether it was driving me around town to local riverbanks to pursue trout, to nearby coves to chase perch and bass, or driving hours every weekend to allow me to work on charter boats, they always encouraged my passion for fishing. Without their love and support I would never have had many of the opportunities that I did to fish. Thank you for everything!

INTRODUCTION

Fishing is a sport, a hobby, a past time, and for some a job. For many it's a passion and for others a way to get away from the hustle and relax. No matter which category we fall into, we would probably all agree that one thing all fisherman are constantly seeking is that special lure or rig that seems like magic and just flat out catches fish. I'm sure this quest will go on until the very last fish on the planet is caught. While I'm not sure about the "magic" part of it, the "umbrella rig", which is the subject of this book, is one rig that I would certainly nominate for being near the top in my arsenal. I have not seen any other lure or rig come remotely close to producing the volume of fish that the umbrella rig has. Not only that, but its' very design and concept often provokes fish to strike by honing in on several key fish behaviors.

Let's start with a description of just what the "Umbrella rig" is and some observations about it. If I had to come up with a strict definition for it, I would phrase it up something like: **The umbrella rig is a multi-dimensional, artificial fishing rig that is intended to imitate a school of bait.**

By design, the umbrella rig has some form of solid center with an eye for attaching your line to. From this center it has multiple metal arms that stick out on the sides. Multiple teasers and/or lures are attached to the arms. This is where the rig gets its name. The frame (the center and its arms) looks like the frame for a typical rain umbrella. A typical umbrella rig might have 5 or 6 teasers (baits without hooks) and three or four baits with hooks (hook baits). By spreading out multiple teasers and hook baits along the arms, the entire setup resembles a school of baitfish when the rig is trolled or reeled through the water.

Before we go any further though, I'm going to stop and answer upfront the question some of you may already have brewing: "If the rig has three or four baits with hooks, does that mean you can catch multiple fish on it at once?"

I put this in quotes because when working as a mate or while running my own boat, I was repeatedly asked if you could catch more than one fish at a time. This scenario played itself out each and every single time a new person was aboard and first saw the rig. The answer:

"YES! You can indeed catch multiple fish at one time with this rig".

A trio of stripers that were feeding on sand eels and were duped by an umbrella at the same time – so YES, you can catch multiple fish at once.

While umbrellas all have some sort of wire frame that is core to them, the variations on rigging them out are endless. Here in the northeast we typically fish two main styles in the saltwater: the sand eel design and the shad design. Besides the type of hook bait that you use on the arms, you can vary the colors, create patterns, vary the lengths of the leaders used (if you use any at all), and even vary the size and weight of the rigs. You can fish them close to the surface or you can fish them deep near the bottom on downriggers. You can fish them on mono, braid, lead core, or wire line. You can even cast them now with the Castable Umbrella Rig on the scene.

Umbrellas are also sometimes referred to as "frames," spreaders, or dredges. Most anglers probably view spreaders as the bars used in offshore fishing for tuna and marlin. These spread the baits horizontally in trying to represent a school of bait on the surface. There's also spreaders for flounder fishing that are used to spread two hooks further apart. Umbrellas also spread multiple baits apart so fit into this classification. Dredges may also spread baits or teasers in multiple dimensions. They're usually used below the surface but they're typically heavier and don't have any hooks on them at all. They are towed with heavier gear versus being trolled off a rod and are often used in offshore trolling to act as teasers in attracting marlin or pelagic game fish closer to the boat so that they can then be enticed into taking a hook bait.

So just what is it that makes the umbrella rig so effective? There have been several theories thrown out there, and probably at least a part of all of them are true. Because the rig appears as a school of bait instead of a single bait, fish find it more worthwhile to expend energy to pursue. The size of the bait itself is more noticeable and is seen by more fish than a single lure would be. The rig vibrates with 5 to 9 (or more) baits spinning and that too is more than with a single bait and is more readily detected by the lateral line sensors of fish. The rig usually represents some form of prominent local baitfish such as sand eels shad, or bunker so it "matches the hatch," so to speak. The rig can also be set up to mimic wounded bait which has an additional triggering effect.

The umbrella rig is not new nor is it a highly held secret. The saltwater version has been around for over 50 years. Throughout these 50 years it's been improved on. There are several enhancements and variations created for specific situations. The freshwater version, on the other hand, is still relatively new and is still undergoing rapid changes.

Despite its longevity and effectiveness, there are still anglers who shy away from using the umbrella rig because they feel it's complex. Others feel it's too costly, or that it tangles easily. Some never experience its true effectiveness because they make mistakes while fishing with it. Hopefully this book will shed some light on each of these concerns and give the reader an understanding on how to use the rigs to their full potential.

I'll start by covering the two most popular saltwater versions of the rig in detail. I'll explain how to rig them, and how to fish them.

Then we'll look at how to rig and fish the freshwater castable version as well. I'll discuss some of the applicable fish behaviors and theories that are behind this rig's success and give you the reasoning behind my suggested approaches. We'll go into related issues: how to rig your tackle for trolling, tips on trolling, and how to store your gear.

This work is truly my first book and I never imagined I'd write one. I started it because I think there is a gap in existing fishing literature when it comes to the umbrella rig. There are numerous pages on bucktail jigs, flies, plugs, bait fishing, and more. However, I have yet to find anything dedicated solely to one of the most effective rigs of all. With the hope of doing some justice to this great rig, I began this book. It may not find its way onto any national best seller list, but my hope is that it will serve as a solid resource for many fellow fisherman interested in how to effectively rig it, and how to fish it successfully.

So without further ado, let's get underway with some discussion on rigging and fishing.

History of the Umbrella Rig

Everything I've read suggests the umbrella rig was invented in the late 1950's by John Sekora (Capt. John), a charter captain who fished out of Montauk, on Long Island, NY. I was able to track down and speak with his son Stephen Sekora and get the real story on the rig's origin. Stephen shared with me some great memories and the story of how the rig really came to fruition. While no murder mystery, it has the vibes of an international spy story.

In the early 1960's, a Captain Gus Pitts of the *MARIE III* and his mate Davey had been greatly out-fishing all of the other boats berthed in Montauk. They were fishing nearby the other boats, fishing less rods, not putting in significantly more hours, but they were catching tremendously better. Captain Pitts' success continued for a couple of years until everyone became very suspicious of him. Rumor had it that some secret lure or technique was being used. It got to the point that there were even a few attempts to break into his boat and see if they could find such a lure or any evidence of his doings.

Little did they know that Pitts and his mate took their lures home with them every night in a black briefcase - a precaution should such an event occur. Captains even tried hiring out of town guys to charter Pitts for a few days so that they could find out exactly what he was doing.

While working aboard another local charter boat, Stephen Sekora remembers a day where they were fishing close to Pitts and the captain decided to run over one of Pitts lines knowing he had some hardware sticking off the hull that would snag Pitts' line. He might then possibly get a look at what Pitts was fishing with. Low and behold he found a straight leader with several wire droppers coming off of it with tube baits. Needless to say that Captain Pitts wasn't happy about the incident.

It happens that during this same time period the menhaden supply around Montauk had dropped dramatically as a result of heavy fishing pressure. The sand eel had become the new primary forage of stripers and blues. Pitts' contraption better emulated the new primary forage rather than the traditional bunker spoons or jigs that everyone else was still fishing with. Pitts later told Stephen Sekora (then around age 13) that on a visit home to visit relatives in Finland, he had seen people fishing for smelt in the local rivers. They had a wire contraption with three arms that had pieces of colored yarn hanging off and containing tiny hooks with which they would catch multiple smelt at once.

Once the news about what Pitts was fishing with got out, everyone in the area began trying to make similar setups with everything from coat hangers to wire leader material. Later on, while aboard a competitor's boat, Sekora inadvertently discovered a picture of a gentlemen on Pitts' boat holding a wire frame with three large stripers hanging off it. Sekora knew what he had seen.

Discussing it with his father, they made several prototypes and would test them each day on their charters, refining them as they learned what worked and what didn't. Initially, they put wire leader material into holes drilled in lead drails and then twisted them with a screwdriver. Later they developed an easier process with a mold. They discovered that the teasers didn't spin around the frame arm if they were in loops on the arm and found that bead chain swivels would reduce the number of tangles and promoted better action.

Sekora indicated that early versions also had long five to six foot leaders under the premise that the wire frames would make fish shy. This proved wrong, and the long leaders were very cumbersome to fish, especially if it was windy. Eventually they developed the four arm frame and began selling it to the other boats, including to Pitts. A few years later, a magazine article appeared about the umbrella and Capt. John told his sons that they needed to act now to begin marketing it, "before someone stole their thunder." In 1967, they started marketing under the name Sekora Lures. They sold it to tackle shops with Capt. John's second son, Grant Sekora, directing the production efforts.

Sekora says his father, "Didn't invent the umbrella rig, but rather he was the original developer of it" The company's mainstay product was the four arm version with a hook on each arm, a four foot leader down the middle, and a fifth lure. Sekora remembers that in order to be able to order a specific hook from Eagle Claw (large but soft that best suited the bend needed for the rigs) they had to place the initial order for at least a million hooks.

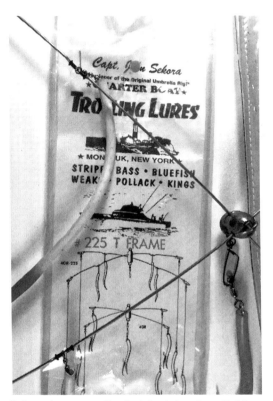

Sekora lures was the "original developer" of the umbrella rig.

Other small shops and manufacturers offered umbrellas of their own but Sekora Lures became the recognized name. Sekora recalls some other manufacturers would actually walk right into their shop to check out what they were doing in hopes of copying their designs.

Through the years several prominent skippers continued to make enhancements to the frame designs, the rigging, and the setup of the umbrellas. Several of the enhancements worked extremely well and stuck as essential components to the rigs that we use today. One of those skippers was from Niantic, Connecticut by the likes of Captain Joe Wysocki, who ran the charter boat *OSPREY* for many years. Joe started fishing and experimenting with these rigs in 1962 and builds a quality frame that is offered at many local tackle shops in New England. He tells me that he used to fish the rigs in his pool to be able to watch them work and figure out how to get the best action from them.

Captain Alan Anderson of Narragansett, RI, skipper of the charter boat *PROWLER* fished umbrellas quite a bit and was well known for fishing them on downriggers for Cod and Pollock in the 1980's. He also tweaked Joe's frames throughout the years, making a miniature version used during extensive striped bass fishing to tag thousands of fish. Al cut the frames down shorter and downsized the hooks, leaders, and tubing to make them more fishable in the Thames River and in salt ponds. In discussing the history of the rig in the Rhode Island area, Anderson indicated that there was one charter boat in the area that seemed to be in on the secret first, the *MAKO II* which was run by Captain Robert Linton and his mate Albert Conti.

I've also heard that the rig made some notable appearances off the islands in Massachusetts during this time frame, but I couldn't find any documentation about who fished them or what was used.

Today there are several manufacturers and many variations of these lures. A freshwater variation broke on the scene hot and heavy around 2011. It is called the Castable Umbrella Rig (CUR) and is often referred to by the name of the original make: "The Alabama Rig." By most accounts this version was invented by Andy Poss from Muscle Shoals, Alabama. The beauty of this version is that it is extremely light (weighed in at about 3/8 oz. before hook baits are attached) and it doesn't have any leaders so it and can be cast without tangling up. It is a plastic body in the center and 5 wire arms come off of it at different angles. Hard or soft baits are attached directly to tiny snaps at the end of the wire arms. While Poss certainly deserves credit for the CUR, some say that freshwater bass pros used variations of umbrellas that date back to the late 1980's, but they were able to keep their secret safe. I have no proof of this though and so I'll leave it at that.

Paul Elias, a professional freshwater bass fisherman, won the FLW Tour Open (Fishing League Worldwide) on Lake Guntersville with Poss's Alabama Rig in 2011. He was on a hot pattern with the lure fishing areas with deeply suspended bass and was blowing away the competition. After just two days he had already caught an amount that some thought might be enough to win the tournament outright – 55lbs. He finished the four day tournament with a bag of 102 lbs. 8 Oz, a weight that was more than 15lbs ahead of the closest competitor. Interestingly, the second place finisher was Bob Behrle who also fished the Alabama rig.

Paul Elias busted open the freshwater scene for umbrellas with his 2011 FLW win. (Photo Courtesy of FLW)

Another very popular variation of this lure is the shad rig which is essentially an umbrella frame with numerous soft plastic shad bodies – some teasers and some hook baits. Every year brings more and more variations as more anglers use these rigs to improve their success. There's a miniature version referred to as a 'kayak umbrella' designed to be trolled off of kayaks and a 'finesse umbrella' that is a lightweight version of the castable umbrella. The latter version is smaller and meant for added flexibility in freshwater. Salmon trollers are also beginning to use frames with spinners as a means of attracting salmon.

While originally developed as a lure for striped bass and bluefish, it also caught some Pollock in the rips as well. In the 1980's when there was a strong Pollock bite in southern New England the umbrella was a key weapon since it keyed in on the prime forage of the Pollock–the sand eel. Fished on downriggers and slow trolled off the bottom, it was not uncommon to hook three or four 30-40lb Pollock at once. Heavy tackle in the neighborhood of 50lb class gear was needed to wrestle this many large fish at once. When the frames came up they were often bent in different directions and they needed considerable straightening.

Umbrella rigs fished on downriggers were deadly on Pollock in the 1980's.

My personal introduction to this lure came at age twelve while fishing with my father in our family boat off the coast of Rhode Island. After hearing numerous fisherman speak to its success, I had to give it a try. That first day we only caught a bluefish or two with it, but it symbolized something more – the start of a long term respect for a rig that simply worked. While I had much to learn about how to use it, how to tune it up to make it more effective, and how to fish it, I was already convinced of its effectiveness.

I began to work as a mate on local charter boats, and over time I got a tremendous amount of experience using this rig. I learned how to handle it, tune it, and exactly how to untangle it in a hurry, especially under the pressure of a screaming captain! This was great experience, and I was fortunate in that I was able to work for and learn from some very good charter skippers including the likes of Captain Al Anderson and Captain Leo Poulin.

Capt. Al was especially proficient with the umbrella rig and meticulous in how he rigged them. He shared his knowledge in many articles, and I've yet to fish with anyone who fishes them more effectively.

Throughout the years I've caught a multitude of species with this lure including striped bass, bluefish, bonita, cod, pollock, weakfish, false albacore, fluke, and sea bass. I've even managed to catch myself with it a few times. I've seen many things that work well with the rigs and have come across a few ideas that didn't pan out so well. I've heard many an angler praise the rig and many curse it, the later most often because they didn't understand how to fish it effectively.

The one thing that the history of the rig embodies is constant experimentation and an endless chain of improvements. As with many great innovations, the umbrella rig began with one person's idea and one purpose in mind. It continued to morph as others become aware of it, and its uses continue to grow.

It pays to watch what others are doing – even if in a different fishery. Pitts took an idea from smelt fisherman in a river in Finland and applied it for his needs to the rips off Montauk. Others improved on his innovation. Freshwater anglers then picked up on what the saltwater anglers were doing and adapted it to their fishery.

The umbrella rig is still evolving, and is one of the more popular, most effective lures used today. Let's dive in to it's current use and discover how to rig, tune, and use it efficiently in your own fishery.

Fish Behaviors and Theories

B efore we begin to discuss how to rig umbrellas and fish them, let's
look at a few of the behaviors of fish that are critical to understanding why umbrellas work so well and why certain rigging or tuning techniques can improve their effectiveness.

If you've spent serious time by the water, even just standing on a dock, at some point you may have come across schools of baitfish swimming together in unison. You may even have marveled at how close they can swim together without running into each other. This amazement is magnified after watching them swim straight together for several yards and then almost instantaneously, they all turn in perfect unison in a sharp zig to the left and a zag back to the right. The reason they don't run into each other is due to a sense they receive from their lateral line. The lateral line is a series of nerve endings along the length of their body that allows them to detect pressure waves coming through the water. Think of the way we humans receive sounds. Through this sensory fish detect fellow members of their school and also the presence of predators.

Scientific studies have shown that when the lateral lines on fish are disturbed the fish will actually collide with one another. Predator fish, such as bass, whether the striped, largemouth, or smallmouth variety, also rely on their lateral lines to "hear" both predators and prey. Bass often rely on this sense before their sight sense kicks in as a means of early detection of a possible meal. Since sound travels up to four times faster in water, these fish "hear" things before their vision or other senses confirm the object. It's the reverse of how humans operate. Vision is usually our first indicator.

Why do these bait fish school together to begin with? The answer lies in the need for self-preservation. First, by swimming together they create an overall larger vibration sensed by other fish. That can fool predators who may perceive of them as a larger, more formidable fish. The second reason, which I find more persuasive, is that by swimming together each individual bait fish is harder to pick out and zero in on than if one or two fish swim together. The tighter they congregate together, the harder it is for predators to focus on and attack one specific baitfish.

Fish school as a defensive behavior so that individuals are less likely to be picked out. Photo by Mike Laptew at Laptew Productions
https://www.mikelaptewfineartimages.com

You may have seen bait schools "ball up" together so close that they literally look like a spinning ball in the water as in the photo above. If you've never seen this before, you should search the internet for life-like video representations. It's amazing to watch. The fish can become so packed together that it's even hard to tell what they are. I've had customers on the boat who thought the water was "muddy" only to realize the brown color was bait packed so tightly that the water looked discolored.

CURs and umbrellas work so well because
they resemble a school of bait.

What happens when a few baitfish are injured or fall behind the rest of the school? You guessed it – they're usually eaten because they're easier targets to single out from the safety of the school, and they become a prime target. Predator fish will often swim through these bait balls – not necessarily to grab a specific bait, but to try to injure or separate individual fish and then pick them off. Injured baitfish are more discernible than the rest of the school, and they send off a more easily distinguished vibration compared to healthy baitfish. The lateral lines of predator fish pick this up and draws them right to the target.

How does this relate to the umbrella rig? Remember that the umbrella rig is designed to imitate a school of bait. In doing so it creates a larger vibration than a single bait so fish pick it up from further away. There's a theory among fishery scientists called "Optimal Foraging." The theory states that a fish wants to get the most rewarding meal while exerting the least amount of effort (or energy). In other words a fish will choose to expend the same energy to get bigger bait or to go after a school of bait rather than to go after single bait where the success rate is lower. So the umbrella, by mimicking a school, appears more rewarding to gamefish.

To make our rigs even more effective, I'll usually have one or two baits that are rigged further back from the others. These will be singled out and/ or will appear wounded as if falling behind the school. These are the ones that should have hooks. It's guaranteed that you will catch most of your fish on the bait rigged further back. When fishing umbrellas with baits on leaders from the frame, I'll purposely make one leader about 10-12" longer than the rest for this very reason. Studies show this configuration will provoke more strikes. It's as if the fish can't resist an injured victim. Other lures have tried variations of the wounded bait theory, but the one that looks like it trails the school works best.

Another fish feeding behavior you can take advantage of is that fish evidence competitive behavior. When fish see another fish chasing a bait down, they'll become competitive. Often they will also try and chase a bait down, or they may even try to catch the same one. If you were to fish some type of larger bait in the rear, or some type of swimming plug, you might produce the appearance of another fish chasing down the bait school. That may elicit strikes on either the plug or umbrella baits. (It's a fish eat fish world.)

Some baitfish have the ability to change colors at times. Some fish can change color to communicate or signal danger or to try and disguise themselves from predators. While this is a secondary consideration, some anglers prefer to use at least one bait that is a different color from the others to make it stand out. The assumption is that doing so creates something for the fish to lock in on as they target your rig.

While I experiment with color combinations, about the only color pattern I'll avoid is a bait with vertical stripes. Vertical stripes, especially in black and yellow, tend to symbolize things that are poisonous or dangerous in nature. This color banding allows them to stand out and is a defense mechanism that warns off predators (fish looking for bait).

Throughout the years I've heard lots of discussion about color vision in fishes and what color lure works best. Some will argue that the color makes no difference. Others argue that the color makes all the difference. I think the color makes a difference in SOME instances. I've had days while trolling for striped bass where a red lure was catching well and the green lure on the other side of the boat was catching just as well. However I've had other days when you couldn't catch fish on anything but green, and other days where you couldn't buy a bite unless it was on blood red colored lures. It appears there are indeed times that color matters.

The one thing that most anglers will agree on, whether in fresh or salt-water, is that in low light conditions, use darker colors, and when there's brighter light, use lighter colored lures. I also like to use brighter color lures when the water is dirtier or stained. It helps the lures be more visible.

I don't think that there is a magical color that works all the time. I usually start off fishing multiple colors until I see that one is catching significantly better than another – or not.

When the water is dirty, freshwater anglers tend to fish a frame that has blades attached. It gives them more play off of the frame vibration and helps make up for the decreased importance of a lure's color.

Keep in mind that the eyes of predators (large fish) usually adjust to changing light conditions quicker than the eyes of their prey. That's one reason a quick storm or dawn/dusk is a prime time to be fishing.

While considering your choice of bait colors is important to your success with umbrellas, the frame options are even more important. Let's consider the range of frame options and the benefits of each.

THE FRAMES

The core of every umbrella rig, whether for freshwater or saltwater use, is the frame. This is the central piece that ties the whole rig together and provides the physical strength of the rig itself.

The center point of the frame is usually some type of weighted or resin body with an eye to which you attach your fishing line. The frame "arms" extend out from the central body and are usually made of some type of metal wire or bar to which the teasers, leaders, and/or hook baits are attached. The arms spread the baits apart and giving it size, thus helping to create the image of a school of baitfish.

The frames themselves are made with various size arms and of various types of metal. Arm lengths, strengths and angles vary. Saltwater versions tend to use stainless steel for their arms with gauges between 11 and 15 (0.075 to 0.125). Freshwater versions can use lighter materials made of bronze, stainless steel, or titanium and of smaller gauges (thickness) such as between 0.021 and 0.051.

The center of the frame has an eye to connect to the umbrella rig. This one has a lead center for added weight and depth.

The centers may be created from different kinds of materials. Saltwater versions commonly are weighted for achieving depth and are usually made of a heavy material such as lead. Freshwater or Castable Umbrella Rigs need to be much lighter so they may have a center constructed of epoxy or plastic. Regardless of style, the center piece will usually have an eye on the front in order to attach your line. It may or may not have a second eye on the backside to which you could attach a teaser or hook bait.

Castable Umbrella rigs usually have a lightweight center that is often molded as a bait body.

Construction of the frame arms will often be straight but some brands may have loops or bends which can be used to attach additional teasers to. Teasers and or hook baits usually can't spin around the arm when attached to these loops. The arm prevents them from spinning, so you may have more tangles and less action from them. You also need to be careful with frames that come with built in loops bent into the arms because over time they tend to get weak at those points. I have had a few break at the loops when some rather large fish jumped on.

I prefer the straight-armed versions for this reason, but there are always exceptions. Rigs built with heavy-duty frames, such as those that are built specifically to fish rubber shads, are built strong enough where the loops don't matter. I've used some of these specifically for fishing shad rigs and have had great success. The shad rigs have much more strain, and the heavy duty frames simply work better. Just because there are no loops in the arms does not mean you can't still attach teasers to the straight-arm models. With other hardware, like a pair of crimps and a swivel, you can attach teasers anywhere along those arms.

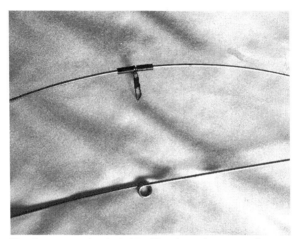

Top frame arm is straight with crimped on snap for attaching teasers. Bottom arm has a loop formed for attaching teasers

As you look into purchasing umbrella frames you'll find many variations in the available arm styles. I've seen some with as many as eight arms and as few as two.

Typically four arms is the old standard on saltwater versions and five was the starting point for CURs.

Freshwater rigs vary regarding the number of arms, determined in part by regulations the different states have enacted.

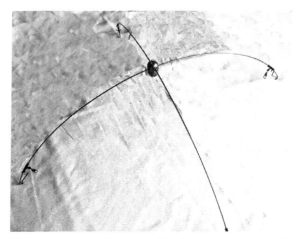

You can see how the umbrella rig gets its name as it looks like the frame of a rain umbrella. This is the four arm model I use most often. It's made by Capt. Joe Wysocki.

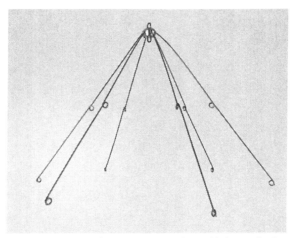

Here's a six arm, heavy duty version with loops in the middle of the arms and the ends. This version is made by 9ers Lures. It works extremely well with shad style baits.

Usually at the end of the arm there is some type of snap or loop where you can either directly attach a bait or attach a swivel with a leader and then a bait. Again, for saltwater I prefer the later. It not only makes the bait school appear larger, but it creates some flexibility in the setup. A 20" piece of monofilament leader is a lot more flexible with a fish jumping around than a stiff wire arm is. I also find that you lose less fish due to "pulled hooks" this way, and it keeps the hook baits further from the metal arms which reduces "spooking" potential bites.

Some ends come as loops – the use of a split ring will let you attach components.

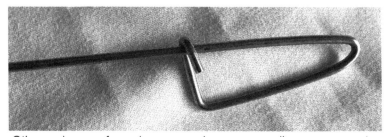

Other ends come formed as snaps where you can clip on components.

CURs usually attach the hook baits directly to the ends of the arms. Since these are meant to cast you don't want leaders that get tangled up each time.

This represents the core construction features of the umbrella frame itself. The remaining components consist of any leaders, teasers, and hook baits. "Teasers" are essentially hook-less baits attached to help create the look of a larger school. They may be slightly different than your hook baits or they may be the exact same bait as your hook bait but without the hook. The last thing you want is to put a hook in every spot on the rig and end up hooking nine fish. Or worse, you could hook three or four fish and then get yourself hooked on one of the extras as you bring your catch aboard. Trust me, you don't want to be hooked by a lure that is also hooked to flopping fish!

I refer to "hook baits" as the lures with hooks in them that are intended to do the actual catching. Leaders are a length of wire or monofilament line that connect the hook baits to the arms of the umbrella. Hook baits usually trail a short distance behind the teasers and are the ones the fish bite. I tend to use monofilament leaders on my saltwater rigs (usually an 80 lb. test-rated line of a low visibility color). I've seen wire leaders and ones made with heavy-duty leader material which will hold up better than the monofilament ones and may also be less prone to tangling. However, I don't prefer them for several reasons:

1. They tend to be a little more expensive.

2. They are usually either more difficult to tie knots with or need to be crimped on. This is fine when you're constructing them at home on a workbench, but when you're in a rocking boat and the bite is going off, you don't want to be messing with tiny crimps and crimping pliers to make a repair. The best alternative for using these type of leaders and getting around this difficult aspect is to carry several pre-made leaders that you can simply clip on as needed.

3. Finally, I also believe the monofilament is less visible to leader-shy fish.

Keep in mind here that there is no right or wrong way. It's purely personal choice.

SALTWATER UMBRELLA COMPONENTS DIAGRAM

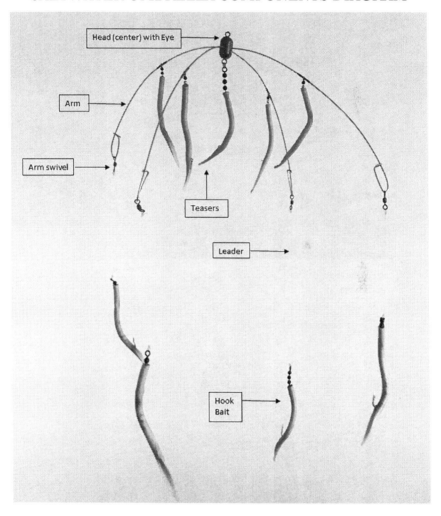

CASTABLE UMBRELLA RIG COMPONENTS DIAGRAM
(Photo courtesy of Picasso Baits, LLC)

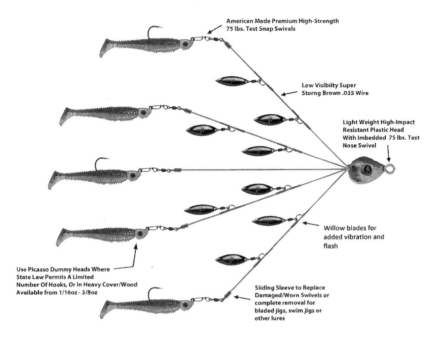

The overall size of the frames matters. The whole purpose of this lure was to imitate a school of bait as opposed to just one. If that's the case, then wouldn't the bigger the frame mean the bigger the school and in turn more attraction? That's potentially true, but there are also practicalities to keep in mind.

Since you're fishing with a rod and reel, you have to have sturdy enough tackle for either trolling these rigs or to take the wear and tear of casting them for a full day. Bigger frames, more teasers or baits, and larger baits all increase the weight and drag of the rig and therefore require the use of heavier tackle. A heavier lure load also means more hardware is in the way when you hook up and while you're fighting your fish and the less flexible it's going to be. I tend to keep my tackle on the lighter side, but I'm always trying to strike a balance between spreading enough baits and keeping my rig light and flexible. That balance is the key.

The largest frame I fish is 25-26" in total diameter and the smaller version is the same frame but reduced in size to 12-13" in total diameter. These frames are made by Joe Wysocki of Osprey Tackle in Niantic, CT and is known for its quality. You can find his frames at most good tackle shops in southern New England.

There are also a few brands of smaller umbrellas out there including styles built for fishing from kayaks. These have shorter arms and usually consist of four baits connected directly to the end of the arms plus one that runs longer down the middle on a leader.

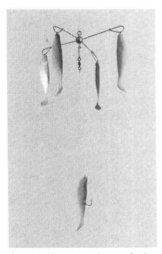

A smaller version of the umbrella that can be used by kayakers

The general rule for CURs is that the bigger they are, the more difficult they will be to cast. Larger CURs also means a larger splash when they land. Poor casting and big splashes don't bode well in freshwater fishing where finesse is a large part of the game. For that reason, keep the CURs to the smallest possible size for the bait style and number of baits that you want. Optimize!

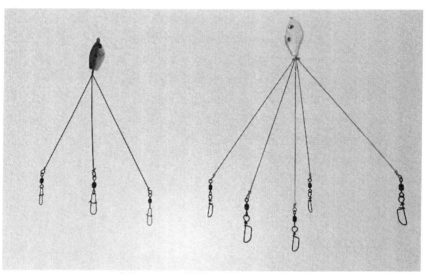

A three arm CUR and five arm CUR

A multiple frame CUR. (Photo courtesy of Shanes Baits)

CURs also come in a multi-frame style. Shane's Baits makes a double-framed version that can get loaded with baits and represent a massive school of bait.

CURs also have a variety of arm styles. Some simply have a swivel or loop fixed at the end to which you would attach your hook baits. Others have a collar that slides and let you change up the swivels if you need to. More sophisticated versions let you change the arms if you were to break one off.

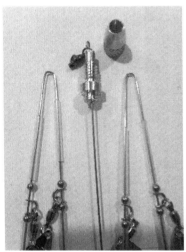

A shot of a uniquely designed CUR with replaceable components (Photo courtesy of Shanes Baits)

Shortening the Arms

I create my smaller versions from the same frame I use for my larger ones. I simply cut the ends off of each arm so that the new length is 8.5" to 9" from the center weight. If the teaser swivels are put on with crimps, you can usually loosen them by squeezing hard with a good pair of pliers. Squeeze on the side of the crimp without the crimp marks, and that should help loosen the crimp. Then slide them into their new positions.

Once everything is repositioned, the crimps can be re-crimped. Change any hardware for teasers that you need to, and remember that you can no longer get crimps on once the frame ends are bent. Then re-bend the end of the arms so that they are in a snap form. When finished the arm lengths are 6-7" so the rig is only about 12-13" in total diameter.

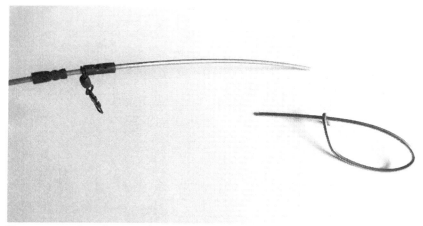

Frames can be shortened to smaller versions by cutting off the ends and re-forming them at a shorter length.

Bending the Frame Ends into Clips

If you get the frames without the ends pre-formed, or you want to cut them down to smaller versions, I'll cover how to bend the ends so that they are essentially a clip you can open or close. Before you begin though, you want to make sure you've added any swivels or crimps on the arm inside of the clip. Once you bend it you won't be able to slide crimps or anything tight on them.

The first step is to bend the last ½" of the tip 180 degrees to the side so that the very tip points back towards the center and is even with the arm itself.

The next step is to go about 1/2" or so in from the bend and bend it 90 degrees downward.

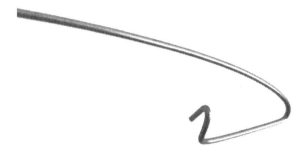

Then you're going to about 1 ¼" to 1 ¾" in from the bend and bend downward again so that the very first bend now fits snugly over the arm.

Okay. So you have set up your frame just the way you'd like it. Now let's have a look at our options for lures, depending on when and where you'll be using them.

THE SAND EEL VERSION

It was a foggy Saturday morning and we were approaching the mussel bars near Matunuck, Rhode Island. I pulled back on the throttle and gave the motion to the crew to go ahead and deploy the rigs. They quickly sprang to life. A green sand eel style umbrella went over the gunnel on the starboard side of the *SHEARWATER* and a fluorescent red version went over the port side.

As the 100' marks on the lines reached the rod tips, the crew locked the reels into gear, leaving the marked sections of Dacron resting in the rod tips. The rods were put into the rod riggers and quickly clipped with the safety lines so that they wouldn't disappear. As we approached the peak of the bar, the depth sounder showed some nice red marks and a few clouds of bait.

"It's looking good guys".

A few seconds later and the starboard rod doubled over and started bouncing indicating that something below grabbed hold. As soon as I put the boat into a starboard turn the port rod also doubled over.

"Doubled up!"

As the anglers maneuvered around the cockpit, switching positions on occasions, the red rig could be seen getting close to the boat. Stepping towards the transom with a pair of gloves I reached down, grabbed the leader, and then took hold of the center of the rig. I lifted high and swung the fish aboard as two 24" sized striped bass flopped onto the deck.

The rod with the green rig still had a ways to go. As that angler continued to work his fish to the boat, the first two fish were quickly measured, tagged with yellow tags from the American Littoral Society, and released over the side.

"He's getting close now" shouted the other angler as his fish approached the boat. Recognizing that this was a bigger fish, I grabbed the net and positioned myself in front of the angler. As the leader came up I saw one large bass and another somewhat smaller one. I dipped the net and made sure I had the larger of the two. Then with one hand holding the net, I reached down with the other and grabbed the leader between the smaller fish and the umbrella frame. Lifting all together, they landed on the deck with a thud.

"Whoa, now that's a bass" shouted the angler who had caught the earlier two fish.

We quickly unhooked the fish. The smaller bass measured 25" and was quickly tagged and released. The other fish measured 42" and the angler decided to keep it. After a couple of quick photos while the fish still had all its beautiful colors, we bled it quickly and put it on ice in the cooler. I helped the second angler untangle his rig, then moved back to the console and slowly put the boat in gear.

"Ok guys, let me spin her around, and then let's get those rigs right back out and see if there are any more".

Before the angler on the port side could get his rig all the way out to the 100' mark, the line started jumping off the spool.

"Hey Cap, I got one already!"

Putting the reel in gear, he started fighting his fish. A few seconds later it could be seen jumping and splashing on the surface – a usual indication of a Bluefish. As we lifted it into the boat, it decided to spill its breakfast all over the back deck. There were pieces of sand eels now all over the cockpit.

"I guess we know what they're feeding on."

"You got it, and that's exactly why we're using these lures," I explained.

As soon as the fish was tagged, measured, and released we headed back to the spot where we started. As soon as the machine started to show the peak of the bar, both rods doubled over again. This action repeated itself over and over again for about two hours until the tide dropped off and the action died. As the tag cards were tallied up, 25 bass and 9 bluefish were counted. Each swam away with a tag identifying them as catches of the *SHEARWATER* that morning.

In addition, two bass and two bluefish rested in the cooler for the crew to take home and enjoy. All of this action took place on sand eel versions of umbrella rigs, fished on a mere 100' of wire line and less than a mile from shore.

Frank Tobin with a nice bass trolled up on a green sand eel version of the umbrella

The sand eel version of the umbrella rig is probably the version that I use most often because sand eels are a common baitfish where I fish in Rhode Island.

Also known as the Sand Lance (*Ammodytes americanus*), the sand eel is a small baitfish that grows to approximately 7" (averaging 4" to 6" as adults). While it's often referred to as an eel and it swims with an undulating motion like an eel, it's actually not an eel but a fish. Sand eels usually swim in very thick schools comprised of thousands of fish, and, as the name suggests, they are usually found around sandy bottom areas. They can burrow into the sand to hide as an additional defensive ability. They feed mainly on copepods and phytoplankton.

Sand eels are one of the most common baitfish in the Northeast.

While several different types of teasers and baits can be used to mimic sand eels, surgical tubing over Limerick style hooks is the most popular and is one of the least expensive. The 5" to 7" sized baits spin due to bent hooks and create a motion similar to a school of sand eels. When you see a caught fish spitting up sand eels or you observe schools of sand eels in the water, you know what bait to use.

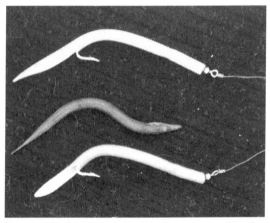

Two surgical tube sand eel baits compared to the real thing.

Before we get into the actual steps of constructing a sand eel umbrella, let's discuss a few of the components and options.

Hooks

Use limerick hooks when creating sand eel versions of the umbrella with surgical tubing. I use Mustad Limerick hooks (#31022DT) in sizes 9/0 and 10/0 for my larger versions and downsize to 5/0 or 6/0 hooks for the smaller version of the rig. The Limerick hook comes with a very distinct bend. It has a bend that starts right behind the eye, peaks about 40% of the way down the shank where it then turns back to bend close to where the hook bend starts. In the photo below, the dotted line indicates how the hook deviates from being straight. If you can't get hold of some Limericks, you can create them using some long shanked hooks and a vise. Just make sure the material the hook is made out of allows it to bend without breaking.

Notice the distinct bend that gives these Limerick hooks their spinning action.

The bend helps give these baits their spinning motion when trolled. A plain straight hook won't have the same motion. Add the tubing half way down the bend, and it adds another bend to the bait that really makes it undulate in the water.

Swivels

This motion created from the Limerick hook is further enhanced based on the type of swivel you use on your hook. As can be seen in many of my pictures, I use bead chain swivels. I learned this setup from a very wise charter skipper I worked for. The bead chains allow those hooks to spin much better than an ordinary barrel swivel would. They also extend the physical length of the bait. I use 175 lb. test bead chain swivels on my large rigs and 75 lb. test bead chains on my smaller rigs.

I have found that you want to be very careful when purchasing your bead chain swivels. Depending on the manufacturer, these swivels can come with several different style ends. You want the ends that are made out of a curved rounded stock and not from drilled flat stock. The flat stock ends usually have rough edges remaining from the cutting process that are too sharp. When you synch down on your knots, the edges will often cut your leader. If they don't cut it at first, they probably will just when you least want them to - once you get a good fish on.

Stay away from bead chain swivels with ends made of flat stock (Top swivel) as the edges can cut your line when pulled tight. Rounded stock ends (bottom swivel) are the way to go.

Some manufacturers of the larger size swivels use wimpy, undersized ends that pull out too easily. Make sure before you buy that they're the ones you want. You may end up paying slightly more for quality swivels, but at least you won't have to worry about their failure with a good fish on.

Tubing

A variety of tubing material can be used to make hook baits and teasers. I've seen latex, vinyl, and plastic used. What's important is that you need to be able to get the tube around the hook effectively.

I prefer to use a latex tubing. It's soft, easy to work with, and it's able to be colored. Its softness may result in a few more bite marks, and slightly less longevity than some other materials, but I believe that it's soft nature makes it easier for a fish to hold on to when it bites.

For my larger rigs I use (3/8"OD by 1/4" ID) tubing for my teasers and (5/16"OD by 3/16"ID) tubing for my hook baits. It has a 1/16" wall thickness and is very flexible. On the smaller version of the sand eel rig, I'll use (5/16"OD by 3/16"ID) for both teasers and hooks.

Most tackle shops in the Northeast carry similar style tubing in a multitude of colors. You can usually buy it by the foot. Natural latex tubing can also be colored using a dye (I recommend RIT Dyes) if you want an exact color. See my chapter on "Other Helpful Aspects" for the steps necessary to dye tubing. My favorite tube colors for striped bass include blood red, fluorescent green, and fluorescent red, or, of course, whatever color just got bitten!

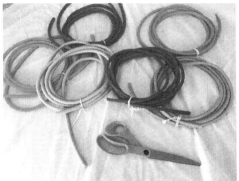

Tubing comes in various colors and sizes. A good sharp pair of scissors is the key to nice clean cuts.

Leader Material

You have several options when it comes to what material to use for your arm leaders (from the arms to the baits). Monofilament, hard leader material, fluorocarbon, and wire will all work. My personal preference is monofilament in the 60-100 lb. test category. If it gets chewed up, it's cheap and can be quickly retied or replaced. While wire and heavy leader material are more resilient to fish teeth and twisting, they are also more time-consuming and expensive to create and replace. I also like the fact that mono is usually less visible and therefore may not scare off as many potential bites.

If you would rather use one of these other materials though, you can get around the difficulty of replacing them at sea by having a couple of pre-made replacements handy. If needed, just unclip the worn one and clip on a new one.

Construction Steps

Starting with the frame, you want to attach the teasers first. I normally put on 5 teasers – one about a third to half way down each arm, and then one behind the center of the frame.

Teasers

I rig my teasers as a #75 lb. test bead chain swivel (4-6 beads) and use some stainless picture hanging wire (19 gauge) to form the bodies and hold the tubing on. You can find the stainless wire at most local hardware stores, and you can easily add a bend, to match the bend of the limerick hook, once you get the tubing over it. I cut a piece of the stainless wire about 7" long and then connect it to one end of the bead chain with a few good twists over itself to keep it on. Next, I'll cut a piece of surgical tubing (5/16"OD by 3/16"ID) that measures from the middle of the swivel and down about 5-6". When cutting the surgical tubing, use a good sharp pair of scissors so that the cut is clean and cut it on a diagonal about one and half to two inches.

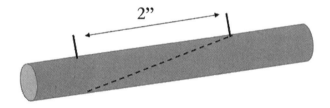

This diagonal is the same kind of cut you'll use for the hook bait and it allows for the hook bend/point to come out, The tubing will continue another two inches or so as a tail. (Note: with a good diagonal cut, you should be able to alternate your cuts to use the remaining half of the diagonal as the tail of your next one.)

Slide the tubing over the wire to cover about half of the beads in the chain swivel. The wire should stick out of the end of the tubing near your diagonal cut. Trim the wire so that you leave about a half inch overhang from where your diagonal cut starts. Using a pair of needle nose pliers, bend the tip (end) of the wire back over toward the swivel so that the point is digging into the tubing ahead of the cut. Make it more of a rounded bend so that the point goes into the tubing. This prevents sharp pokes and helps hold the tubing on while you're trolling.

This completes one teaser. Next, I'll simply attach it to the clip or the split ring on the frame. If your swivel is already on the frame, you can add the wire and tubing directly to that swivel.

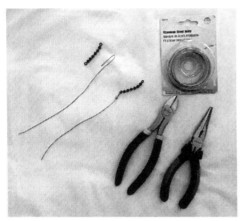

Bead swivels, stainless wire, and a pair of pliers are all you need to create the core of the teaser.

Slide the tubing onto the wire so that the wire comes back out the tail end. Pull the tubing up over the first bead or two to help make it stay on tight.

Trim the wire so that you have about a half inch sticking out.

Bend the wire back over and into the tubing to hold the tubing in place.

Once the teasers are attached to the frame you can give them a bend to match the Limerick hooks. That will help them spin in the water. It's kind of a multi-dimensional bend in that you are going to go both to one side and down.

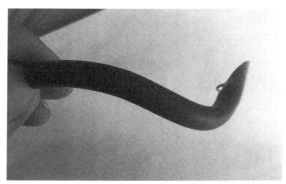

Seek a multi-dimensional bend in your teasers to match those of the hook baits.

Hook Baits

Before you put the tubing on, attach your bead swivels to the hooks. I use a 1 7/8" (175 lb. test) 4 -6 bead chain swivel for the larger rigs and 75 lb test 1 and 3/8" 5 or 6 bead swivel for smaller rigs. To put one of these on, you'll have to slide it into the open eye of the hook and then close the eye with a good heavy pair of pliers or a vice. (Open it in a vice using a screwdriver if it's not already open.)

Now, we need to cut the surgical tubing to create the actual body of the bait. For the large rigs I'll use (3/8" OD tubing) (¼ ID X 1/16 Wall X 3/8 OD LATEX TUBING) and for the smaller rigs I'll use the (5/16" OD tubing)(3/16 ID X 1/16 wall X 5/16 OD LATEX TUBING).

To measure the cut, place the end of the tubing half way down the swivel. Then hold it close against the shank of the hook following the hook to the bottom of the bend. At that very point is where you want to start a diagonal cut (like the one used for the teasers).

After you cut the first one, use it as a template for the rest. You can also do alternating cuts if you make your diagonal cuts clean and decent.

Once you have your hook tubes cut, take one and, starting with the squared off end, slide it over the hook starting at the hook point end.

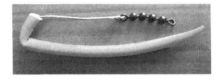

This usually needs to be done with a series of tugs and twists until you work it all the way over the hook and the point comes out were your diagonal cut starts. I like to pull and twist the front end with one hand and push and twist the tail end with the other hand.

Continue pulling it on until the start of the tubing is about half way up the swivel. If done properly you'll still have the diagonal cut end of the tubing slightly bending downward on the bend of the hook shank.

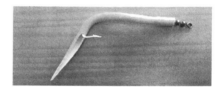

Repeat this process for each of your hook baits, Make sure to have swivels on the tip of each arm to tie your leaders to.

The next step is to cut your leaders and attach them to the hook baits and the end of the frame arms. I use improved clinch knots to make the connections and #80 lb. test mono. You can use mono or use a material like hard leader material or wire. I usually leave one about 12 to 16" longer than the others to create that wounded straggler effect that we talked about earlier.

In lieu of surgical tubes, I've also used red gills on these rigs and have also seen other eel-like baits used such as Hogys, Slug-gos or other forms of tubes. Just make sure whatever you put there has some kind of swimming action. Part of the beauty of this rig is that you have an endless number of ways to rig it up. So keep experimenting.

Additional Options

Some charter captains like Capt. Al Anderson used to use a head on their surge tube baits. Originally a "glow head," a plastic head formed on a bead chain swivel that glowed, was available. This worked great when fishing the rigs deeper for fish like cod and Pollock. ATOM Lures also created a similar style head made of metal called an Action Head. Neither head appears to remain in production, and I've been unable to locate a source for either of them. I can't obtain them even for my own use. Perhaps someone will come up with a similar product made of resin or by using one of the new style fly heads.

You can vary your tube baits with multi-colored tubing, dying one half a different color, or even by using different colored mylar tubing (with a clear tubing over them). See my "Other Helpful Aspects" chapter for dyeing instructions.

Besides using the straight cut tails described earlier, some anglers prefer split tails or shredded tails. I haven't done a lot of experimenting when it comes to the tail style, but I have caught fish on all three lure style.

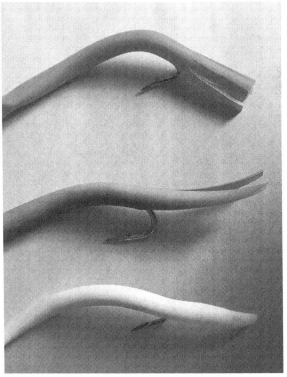

Split or shredded tails (top 2) are another option to the standard tail (bottom).

My personal favorites for colors are blood red, fluorescent green, fluorescent red, natural, and black.

Materials for larger sand-eel version of Umbrella rig	
1	Umbrella Frame
5	75 lb test bead chain swivels for teasers
3'	SS Picture Hanging Wire for teasers
3'	5/16" OD Tubing for Teasers
4	175 lb test bead chain swivels for hook baits
4	8/0, 9/0, or 10/0 Limerick Hooks
3'	3/8" OD Tubing for Hook Baits
4	2/0 or 1/0 swivels for end of arms
10-12'	#80 lb test mono for leaders
1	Stainless Split rings (# 6)
8	Crimps (sized to match arms) - if you need to crimp your teasers on arms.

Materials for smaller sand-eel version of Umbrella rig	
1	Umbrella Frame (10-15" in diameter)
9	75 lb test bead chain swivels for teasers and hook baits
3'	SS Picture Hanging Wire for teasers
6'	5/16" OD Tubing for Teasers and hook baits
4	5/0 or 6/0 Limerick Hooks
4	1/0 swivels for end of arms
8-10'	#80 lb test mono for leaders
1	Stainless Split rings (# 6)
8	Crimps (sized to match arms) – if you need to crimp your teasers on

Common tools for working with umbrella rigs

- Needle nose or good pair pliers
- Heavy pliers or cable cutters for bending arms and/or cutting arms if need to
- Pair of regular wire nippers for cutting leaders, old snaps and swivels, etc.
- Split ring pliers
- Sharp pair of scissors for cutting the tubing, the sharper the better
- Small file or sharpening stone for sharpening hooks

The Shad Bait Version

As we were exiting the harbor we could see peanut bunker flipping and schooling all over the surface, following the ebb currents of the pond out into the sound. Air temperatures were starting to cool dramatically as September was now in the rearview mirror and Halloween was quickly approaching. Occasionally larger splashes could be seen and the tail thump of a larger fish could be heard to go along with it. Gannets were circling above, and when lined up above a school, would commence their dive bombing that resulted in huge splashes as they hit the water in pursuit of the bait. Two shad umbrella rigs were slowly released behind the boat as we slowly eased our way along. Pods of bait could be seen on the depth sounder about 10 feet down with frequent red marks showing below them. Soon the port rod started thumping as drag eased its way off the reel. As the angler held onto the rod, waiting for a chance to gain some line back, the starboard rod bounced abruptly four or five times and then went quiet.

"We better check that rig to make sure it's okay."

Reeling it in quickly, the telltale sign of bluefish could be seen as three of the four hook baits no longer had tails. As spare shad bodies were quickly put in place of the bitten ones, the other angler was getting his fish near the boat.

"The leader's almost here."

Grabbing the net and positioning myself just astern of the angler, color could be seen coming up. A few moments later a nice striped bass was resting in the cockpit, a six inch rubber shad hanging from the corner of its mouth. The boat was put back in gear and pointed towards the circling birds to the southwest. Off our bow the bait drove skyward and rained over the surface only to be met with a series of dive bombing attacks from above by gannets. Both rods doubled over in unison and anglers sprang into action. My cup of coffee was now cold, but who cared, the morning was off to a good start.

Shad bait umbrellas are great options when the fish are feeding on a bigger baitfish such as shad, bunker, herring, or mackerel. Instead of using the tubes like in the sand eel version, you'll substitute rubber shad baits (in whatever style you want) for both the teasers and the baits. I prefer to use shad baits that have a paddle tail which gives them a good swimming action. While you can certainly mold your own rubber baits, I prefer to purchase mine. You can usually find these baits in a variety of color patterns and sizes ranging from 2" up to over 10". I tend to go with the 6" baits for most of the striper trolling I do but may downsize to either the 3" or 4" if I'm seeing that the bait in the area is smaller.

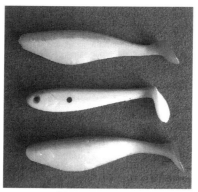
Shad style baits

A word of caution here though – you need to be selective in the use of shad baits in saltwater because if there's a lot of bluefish or other toothy fish in the area these baits simply will not hold up. You'll find that you'll start accumulating chunks of rubber bait heads in the back of your boat, will go through your bag of replacements quickly, and will later need to empty your wallet at the tackle shop to replace them. (By the way, make sure that these plastic chunks find their way into the trash and not into the water!) That all being said, they're tough to beat as an artificial bait when there's a lot of bunker around.

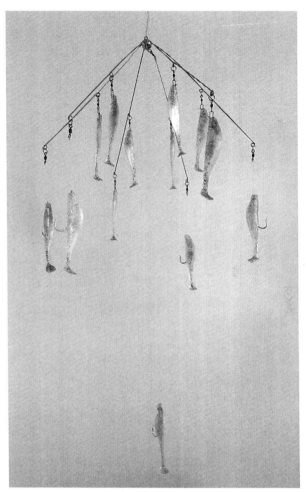

A shad bait version

Rigged on the same frame as my sand eel versions, here's a shad version. Notice one bait trailing all the others.

Teasers

In choosing an umbrella frame with which to pull shad baits, look for something that's somewhat sturdy. As I mentioned there's more drag created from these types of baits, and if your frame arms are too flimsy they'll bend right over; they won't keep your baits as spread apart; and possibly they will even break.

The first step is to put on the teasers. I'll use the combination of a good swivel and a DUOLOCK snap. I use a #1 (150lb test) Barrel swivel and a #56 (150lb test) or #55 (86lb test) DUOLOCK snap. Since the teaser is the same soft plastic bait as the hook baits we can attach the teaser by

48

opening the large end of the Duolock snap, inserting the end of the snap wire into the front of the baits head and then push it through the bait so that it comes out the top of the back (about three quarters of an inch back from the front). After twisting the bait slightly so that it rides flat on the snap, we can close the snap. Presto! That's it.

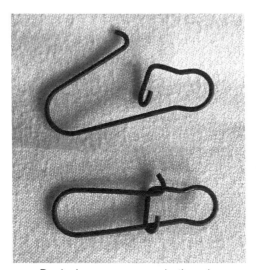

Duolock snaps open on both ends.

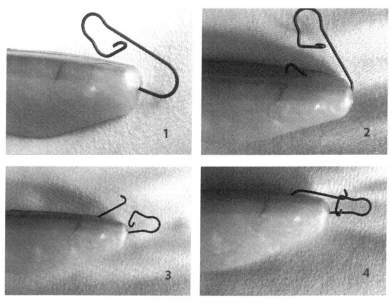

1) The open end of the duolock snap goes in the center of the front of the shad. 2) Push it in so that it comes out the top. 3) Straighten the shad on the duolock so that it rides straight. 4) Lock the duolock.

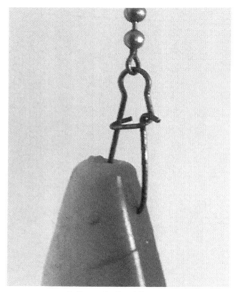

A rigged shad teaser

There are other options to attaching the teasers besides Duolock snaps (1) We could use the stainless picture hanging wire like we did on the sand eel version and start by going through the center of the front of the head, pushing it through the bait a couple of inches, and then coming out top and bending it back onto itself. It's not as clean and is more work if you need to replace one so I usually leave this as method of last resort (2) we could use large bait keepers (screws) or centering pins. These are spring like wires that look like mini corkscrews. They have a loop on one end and a screw like shape on the other and can be literally screwed right into the front of the bait and then connect the loop on front to attach them to a frame or swivel. These work best on freshwater versions because you're dealing with smaller baits usually and clearer water (so we want less hardware showing).

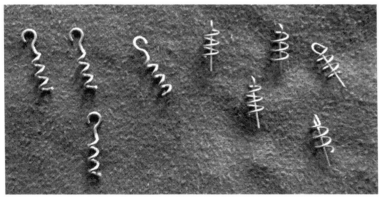

Centering pins are great for attaching shad teasers.

The front part of the Duolock should open as well and you can clip it to whatever swivel, split ring, or snap that you have on your arm. You'll need to repeat this process for however many teasers you want to install.

Hook Baits

The next step is to make sure that you have a swivel on the tip of each arm where you're going to want to attach a leader for your hook baits.

Cut approx. 2-3' sections of mono leader (depending on how long want your leaders) and attach one end of each to a hook with an improved clinch knot (or other knot that you prefer). To add the shad bait to the hook, take one of your rubber shad baits, hold it along the side of the bait with the eye of the hook just at the head of the bait and see where the hook bend would want to come out of the bait on the top. Mark the spot lightly (or hold a finger on it) and then insert the hook point in the front of the baits head and work it back so that it comes out of the bait at that spot that you have marked. Make sure that you do this as straight a path back and then up as you might otherwise end up with a wavy bait which might not want to swim properly. Now work the shad body over the hook so that the eye of the hook is at front and the bait is lying flat on the hook. The hook point should ideally come out roughly half way to two-thirds of the way back on the shad body. Too far back and the bait might bend on the hook or not maintain enough of its action. Not far enough and you may miss bites.

For hooks on a 6" shad rig, , I use a 8/0 or 9/0 #3407 Mustad hook, usually tied directly to the leader. I don't normally add a swivel here because unlike the tubes on the eel version, I don't want these baits to spin but rather to swim. Sometimes I'll use a 2/0 (225lb test) barrel swivel through the eye of the hook, mostly if I have a shorter hook shank that I want to extend for protection against bite offs. To attach the swivel to the hook you may need to open the eye of the hook with a strong screwdriver and vise if it doesn't come open already. Insert the eye of the hook into the vise and tighten to close it back up. For smaller shads I'll down size the hook size to better fit in the bait. For the larger baits (over 6") it's possible that you may even need to pull the eye of the hook and some of the leader into the bait in order to get the hook back far enough.

Now attach the other end of your leader to the swivels on the end of your frame – making sure to adjust the length for how you want. Again, I'll use an improved clinch knot for this and will then trim the tag ends on each end of the leaders.

I like to make one of the leaders about a foot or so longer than the others to give the appearance as if that one baitfish is possibly injured and lagging behind the rest of the bait school. This is usually the one to get the most bites as fish tend to hit the stragglers from the school before hitting the school itself.

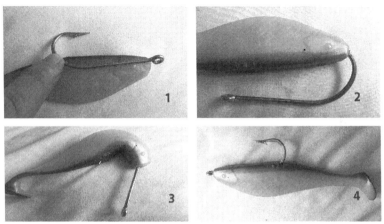

1) Measure up the hook to see where the point wants to come through. 2) start with the hook in the center of the bait's head. 3) insert the hook in a straight line through the bait so it comes out where you measured. 4) Slide the hook all the way up so eye is at front and bait is lying flat on the hook

Again, these rigs will create more drag in the water while being trolled so you may want to step up your tackle to a little heavier gear. This includes using a stiffer rod, a reel with greater line capacity, increased drag, and a higher line strength. You may find that to get the best action from them you also may need to slow the trolling speed just a tad versus other trolling methods.

You can also easily create a variation of this rig by using only one hook bait. All you need to do in order to create this version is attach all teasers (no hook baits, and possibly no leaders) to all of the arms and then run one longer leader down the center (from behind the center of the umbrella frame) and attach your shad hook bait here. This is a great option if you don't want to be fighting multiple fish at a time like when you have younger children fishing with you.

I've seen some fishermen use brighter colors on the baits near the rear on the theory that they represent ones that are lit up more than the ones in the front of the school. By using brighter colors they try to simulate this. I've seen squid do that and see it more prevalent on spreader bars for tuna fishing but have not seen proven results elsewhere. Personally the ones with vertical stripes are pretty much the only ones I make a point to stay away from.

When purchasing your supplies for these make sure to always get a bag of replacement baits to have with you. If you get attacked by some toothy critters along the way (or simply catch so many fish the tails get worn) you can easily replace them and keep fishing.

Bluefish like to bite the tails off of shad baits.

I've included a quick shopping list of the items that you'll need for creating a shad umbrella on your own:

Materials for Shad Bait Version of Umbrella Rig (4 arm)	
1	Heavy Duty Umbrella Frame
4	2/0 swivels for ends of arms
4	8/0 or 9/0 Mustad #3407 hooks or equivalent long shank hooks
9	6" Rubber shad baits (Minimum - Make sure to buy extra as replacements)
5	#55 or #56 Duolock snaps for teasers
5	Stainless Split rings (#10)
12'	#80 lb test mono for leaders

THE CASTABLE UMBRELLA RIG

The Castable Umbrella Rig (CUR), not usually having the leaders and such that the saltwater umbrellas do, is more a matter of choosing your baits and teasers. That however, doesn't mean that just as much thought shouldn't go into rigging them. Your choice of frame will depend on how many baits and teasers that you want to present and how heavy (or light) you want the rig to be. Once set with the frame then you will choose what type of bait you want as the hook baits and teasers.

The CUR when it broke on the scene in 2011. Even since 2011 castable umbrella rigs have come along way. (Photo courtesy of FLW)

Baits

While some CUR manufacturers will sell a complete rig with all components including the jig heads and baits, others allow you to purchase just the frame and add the individual components that you want.

Your bait of choice may impact the jig head type that you select so I would choose your baits before choosing a matching jig head. My personal preference here is a slim, stream lined bait type but it must have some action like a paddle type tail or something. You also want to somewhat match the hatch so to speak by choosing a bait that is somewhat similar to the baitfish in the waters that you'll be fishing. With that all said, there are literally an endless amount of choices. Some of the baits that you may want to consider include:

- Keitech–Swing Impact
- 6th Sense–Core-X Swimbaits
- YUM–Money Minnow
- Manns – Hardnose Shad or Mullet
- Zman – Elaztech PaddlerZ, Pogyz, or swimmers
- Basstrix – Swim baits or paddle tails
- Strike King – Shadalicious
- H&H Lures–Cocahoe Minnow

Swimbaits that come with the weight and head built in can be effective as well. A couple of styles to consider would be:

- Storm – Wildeye
- Tsunami – Holographic swim shads

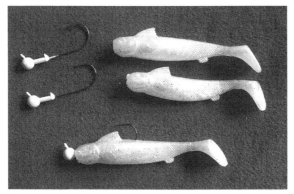

Mann's Hardnose Shad are a popular bait for rigging
on CURs

Fishing CURs on the saltwater side, I've done well with rigging mine up with mini shad type baits as well as Cocahoe Minnow baits. Again, something with a paddle type tail to give them a swimming action.

Paddle tail baits provide great swimming action
on CURs. (Photo Courtesy of FLW)

As I mentioned before, there's almost an endless amount of choices here. I apologize to any manufacturers or brands that I left out – it's certainly not because others may not be effective but rather I only wanted to provide a few examples from personal experiences.

There are also a significant number of options for jig heads and you directly influence the overall weight with the size of the jig heads that you choose. If you need more depth and have the gear heavy enough to toss it with, you can go heavy on the jig heads. If fishing shallow or in more confined spaces you may want to go lighter weight. Most pro anglers are going to carry several rigs with them with varying weights so that they can best match the existing conditions they're facing without having to spend a lot of time re-rigging. This may or may not be feasible for you but it does save time while on the water.

When putting your baits on the jig heads, all the usual tips will apply. If the back of the jig head is flat you may want to trim the front of your bait slightly to match and fit snug. You may also want to trim it slightly to adjust where the hook comes out. Ideally you want the hook as far back in the bait without impeding the swimming ability of the bait. That usually means that you want the hook to come out before (on the front side of) any thin section of the tail. If your jig head does not come with baitholder barbs, you may want to add a touch of some super glue to help keep it from sliding. In general, you also want to make sure that the bait is on the jig head straight so that it swims as designed. If it's on crooked, it may want to swim to the side or spin.

Balancing

In most cases your jig heads are simply going to snap on to the arms directly via the snap swivels at the end. When rigging up your CUR, the key thing to remember is to maintain some balance to the rig so that it runs true. What I mean by this is to try and keep the weight distribution even along the centerline of the rig. For instance, if fishing three jig heads on a five arm rig, don't load all three jig heads to one side or the rig will want to fish off center. Instead, rig one jig head on each side and one down the middle. If you need to vary the weight of the jig heads, again, keep the two side ones somewhat even and vary the center one.

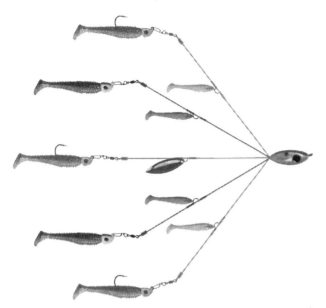

A Picasso CUR. Notice how it's rigged in balance.
(Photo courtesy of Picasso Lures, LLC)

Shane Lehew along with one of his multi-frame castable umbrellas (Photo Courtesy of FLW - /Photographer Gary Mortenson)

When looking at what baits to use, you want to use one that will both somewhat mirror the size and look of the local bait as well as ones that have an inherent swimming action built in. Because you are not working these baits individually, you need them to have some action on their own so that as the rig moves through the water they have a swimming action. Whether it's a curly tail, a paddle tail, or some other feature, they should have some action to them.

If there are extra attaching points, then bait keepers or centering pins can be used to load on plastic bait teasers, as can smaller duolock snaps. Because frequent casting may bounce the rigs around, you may want a dab of a super glue to help keep the plastic bait on and to keep it from sliding off during the cast. The other option for attaching teasers, especially if reducing the number of hook baits due to regulations is to use a "Dummy Head." Essentially it's a jig head but instead of having a hook it has a centering pin to screw the plastic bait on. These are great when you still need the weight of the jig head but have to reduce the number of baits with hooks.

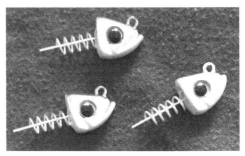

Dummy Heads and centering pins can be used for attaching hookless baits (Teasers).

When setting up a rig that has more arms than hook baits, try and leave the hook baits on the bottom arms and to the outsides. This is where most of your strikes will come so you want to make sure that those are the ones with the hooks.

Some CURs may come with blades or spinners as teasers. These help to create both flash and vibration. If the water is stained or there's a lower level of light present then the added blades may be something to consider. The additional vibration will help the lure get noticed via the fish's lateral lines, and additional flash from the blades will help provide visual reference for the fish to find it. Blades usually need to be attached via some type of clevis or snap that allows them to spin.

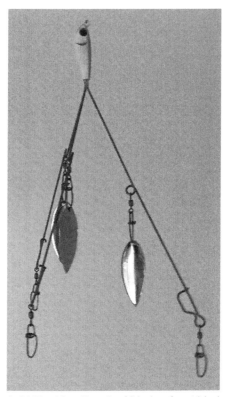

A CUR with willow leaf blades for added flash and vibration

Most CURs will come rubber banded or tied up for smaller packaging. Some may have a circular metal loop used to slide over the arms keeping them together – you may want to snip that off if it keeps sliding down while you are fishing. When you open them up and either start rigging or fishing with them, you'll want to make sure that the arms are all bent at appropriate angles. The packaging may have compressed them tightly together. You want your baits to spread out so they're not touching or tangling and so they simulate a bait school. Remember the arms are made of wire so make sure that you do any bending carefully and slowly.

As mentioned in the section on saltwater fishing, using a different color bait for one of the hook baits may give the fish something to lock onto. As mentioned, schooling behavior is to confuse the predators so making one stand out will sometimes be more effective. You can do this when you rig up by using a different color bait or you may simply adjust one of the existing baits via the use of a paint pen or marker to add some coloring – either a stripe, dot, or whatever.

Always, always, always check the swimming action of your CUR before putting it into action. While this seems so obvious, it is often the most overlooked aspect. If just one of those baits or teasers is not swimming properly it might deter from the entire presentation.

Materials for Castable Umbrella Rig	
1	Frame
3-5	Small jig heads (if extra weight needed and heads for lures)
3-5	Plastic lures or swimbaits with hooks
3-5	Similar style plastic baits with no hooks to use as teasers
4-6	Shaky Heads or bait centering pins

FISHING SALTWATER UMBRELLAS

Saltwater umbrella rigs often seem intimidating to those that haven't used them, but once you've fished with them they're a piece of cake. I'm not sure where the intimidation factor comes from – perhaps its all the leaders and potential tangling. Or maybe folks just don't want to change what they've been doing. However after fishing the rig with someone that knows what they're doing, most people find it easy to use and are convinced of the rig's effectiveness.

Tackle

For Trolling, I like a rod with a flexible tip but also one with enough backbone to handle it when you get a good fish on, or multiple fish. A softer tip helps limit how much the rig jerks around when the boat bounces with the waves. It helps absorb a little motion. Usually you want a rod of at least 6'6" or longer for trolling.

A rod with a lighter tip but plenty of backbone works best.

I use three styles of rods for trolling frames: When trolling in rivers or bays where it's shallow (under 20') and if I'm fishing mini size umbrellas or CURs, I use a lighter 6'6" fluke rod loaded with a level wind reel and lead core line. Along the beaches and in the sound I'll use a 7' wire line rod that is lightweight and loaded with #50 (0.020) Inconel Wire.

When fishing deeper water and using extra trolling weights and possibly heavy shad rigs, I'll fish a rod that's stiffer and in the 30-50 lb. class with carbide guides and #60 (0.025) Inconel wire line.

For reels, I like conventional trolling reels like the Penn 320GTIs, 4/0 Senators, or Penn Fathom 20. When fishing wire, stainless spools work best to help prevent corrosion. Aluminum reel spools and stainless wire line create spool corrosion when water is added. It's getting harder to find good stainless spool reels nowadays, so I will use aluminum spools in some cases, but I always take the line off at the end of the season and clean them well. I still get some pitting, but I can usually keep it to a minimum and make the reel last for several years. Except for the GTI's, I usually end up having to remove the level wind mechanism because the knots on wire line don't always go through them. As opposed to beating the knots up and risking that one could give out, I'd rather simply remove the mechanism.

While saltwater umbrellas work best with wire line or lead-core to help achieve proper depth, the use of monofilament and braid will still allow you to catch with the umbrella. Braid works better than monofilament because the smaller diameter allows it to get deeper. Most monofilaments tend to fish high in the water column, so you may have trouble getting your rigs deep enough. You'll need to use a trolling sinker if using braid or mono. If you're going to the trouble of fishing with umbrellas though, you're really best with wire or lead core.

For fishing in water more than 45 feet deep, use downriggers. Umbrella rigs fish extremely well off downriggers.

If you find that you only need to get a tad deeper than your flat line allows, or if fishing with mono, try a trolling sinker to get your rig deeper. These attach in-line to your line between the umbrella rig and the snap swivel. Keep a couple on board in varying sizes so you can adjust the depth at which that you're fishing. The only caution I'll warn about with trolling sinkers is to make sure you get ones with strong snaps.

Have a few trolling sinkers handy in various sizes in case you need some help getting your rig deeper.

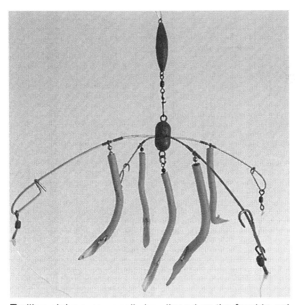

Trolling sinkers can easily be clipped on the front to get more depth.

Fishing the Rigs

Let's walk through some remaining points on fishing umbrellas via a description of a typical fishing trip.

The very first thing we want to do is to get our rigs ready before we arrive. Make sure they're untangled, have no nicks or frays in the leaders, have sharp hooks, that the hook baits ride on the hooks properly and are ready to go. Depending on where we'll be fishing and the conditions of brightness and water clarity, we'll choose our colors or styles and have them ready to go. They'll be clipped on and the reel drags will have been checked.

Upon arriving on the grounds and slowing down to trolling speed, it's time to get the rig in the water. By reeling up so that only a few feet of line exists between the rod tip and the rig, we can swing it carefully over and into the water. The frame leads and the hook baits trail behind.

Don't be afraid to swing the umbrella out to deploy it - just make sure it's not tangled once in the water.

When it hits the water and starts to swim, observe it to make sure it's not tangled and that the lures are running properly. The most common mistake anglers make when using the umbrella rig is failing to make sure the rig is untangled in the water. Why bother to put it out if it's already tangled since it won't catch that way?

With our thumb on the spool, let it out S-L-O-W-L-Y, stopping it every 20 to 25 feet to let it catch up. Failure to do so is another common mistake anglers make fishing these rigs. If we let it out quickly without periodically stopping it to catch up, the frame is likely to sink quicker than the leaders. That causes it to tangle and not be effective. If it sinks too quickly, it can also hit the bottom and become snarled in weed, or worse, hung up.

It's important to keep your thumb on the spool for other reasons as well. Besides controlling the speed of release, a thumb on the reel acts as a temporary drag while the reel is in free spool should you get a bite on the way out. Your thumb also helps keep the wire line from jumping ahead of itself.

Keep your thumb on the spool to prevent backlashing and to act as a temporary drag.

As in most circumstances when trolling, if the boat is in a turn we want to be letting line out from the side of the boat to the outside of the turn so as not to create tangles. (Especially when you are fishing multiple rods, you don't want to let line out from the side of the boat to the inside of a turn. That's a sure recipe for tangled lines.)

I mark my trolling lines with either Dacron sections (on my wire line outfits) or with dental floss (on my lead core outfits). I mark them at pre-measured distances where I'll want to fish them. This helps in several ways. First, I know exactly when to stop letting line out when I reach the right depth. When fishing with guests or clients, I can easily tell them to let it out until they get to the yellow section or the double floss marks, and they will know what I mean. I can also see and confirm that they did set it at the right mark. The Dacron section acts as sort of a shock absorber from the rod tip, thus protecting the sections of wire line as the line wears back in forth in the tip as we troll.

When trolling wire, we make sure that only the Dacron sections are located at the rod tip before we put the reel in gear. Never is the wire left at the tip.

While trolling I like my rods to be set out to the sides, almost in a horizontal position. This keeps the tips low to the water and more of the line in the water. More line in the water allows the rig to fish deeper. The use of rod riggers (or out-rodders) helps to spread the rods apart and keep the tips lower. Rod riggers are simply metal pipe-like fittings that fit into the existing vertical holders in your gunnel and have a holder that positions the rod out to the side. Mine have a pin you can pull out, and the rod holder part will flip up for ease of removal. I clip a safety line to the reel in case any slips occur while someone is getting a rod out, or if we get a bite on a turn when the rod could pull straight out. These work significantly better than simply putting the rod in a vertical holder.

Rodriggers help to spread your lines and keep the tips lower to the water.

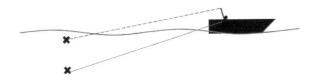

With rod tips nearer the water, more line is in the water
and the rig fishes deeper.

For anglers wanting to hold onto their fishing rods while trolling, it's
helpful to have some type of pins that you can rest the rod against. That
alleviates some of the strain of the rig being trolled. Captain Al Anderson
had these on the *PROWLER* and it was a great way for anglers to feel
more connected in the process and enjoy the impact of a bite. They could
sit in the trolling chairs, hold the rod out to the side and rest it on the
pins. (It's almost the same as using rodriggers.) When they got a fish, they
could simply lift it up, put the butt in the gimbal of the trolling chair,
and start fighting.

While we're trolling, I constantly watch the sounder for signs of bait,
fish, and bottom structure. I'm also scanning the nearby surface for signs
of slicks, birds, and bait. If you mark fish and you are consistently seeing
them at a certain depth, you know where to adjust the depth of your rigs.
Meanwhile, anglers should have at least one person watching the rod tips
who can recognize the signs if the rigs are bouncing the bottom, picking
up weeds, or getting a bite.

You can temporarily adjust the depth of your rigs by varying the speed
of your troll. If I go over a deep spot and mark some fish way down deep,
I might pull the boat out of gear and into neutral for a few moments to
allow the rigs to sink down a little before I put it back in gear. Likewise,
if I come to a jump in the bottom or mark fish up higher, I might bump
my troll speed up a notch to bring the rigs temporarily higher.

I can also adjust one rig up and one rig down by putting the boat in
a turn. If I turn to starboard, the strain on the rod to the starboard side
is going to lighten up and sink a little while the rig on the port side will
speed up and rise.

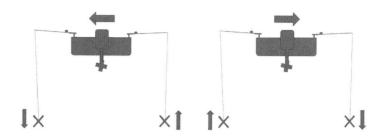

Lines on the outside of the turn will speed up and rise while lines on the inside of the turn will slow and sink.

I always try and pay attention to the direction in which I'm going when we get bites. Am I going with the current or against it? Are the fish only hitting when we're going in one direction, or doesn't it matter? Little clues can add up to a lot of success at the end of the day. In addition, depending on wind, current, and sea state, I'll adjust my trolling speed to the conditions. I can tell my ground speed from my GPS. If I'm working against the current or wind, I might need to bump it up a little to maintain an acceptable speed for the rigs. Likewise, I might need to pull it back some so I don't go too fast when I have these elements working in the same direction.

If you go for some time without getting bites, inspect your rigs periodically for weeds, especially if you see weed in the water when trolling. When fishing a multiple hook rig like the umbrella, you're much more prone more to pick up weeds, and you're not going to get many bites if the rigs are weeded up. If the area has so much weed that you're constantly getting weeded up, you might be better off moving to cleaner water. Watch the rod tip as its trolled. If you see it suddenly bounce and suspect it hit bottom or maybe had a strike, check it shortly afterwards for weeds or tangles.

Weeded up rigs are not going to catch. Check them periodically.

The umbrella rig usually provides all the action necessary when trolled so you do not need to jig it. In fact you shouldn't because it's likely to tangle if you do. I know there's always that old fishing habit that if you jig the rod a few times you'll entice a strike but with these rigs you'll tangle them up and prevent strikes. Save that jigging technique for a bucktail or a bait rig. Watch the rod tip while you're trolling. If it bounces or you suspect it hit bottom, don't hesitate to check it for weeds.

I will often fish a different color on each side of the boat to learn if a pattern exists. The best color is always the last one that caught a fish.

When we get a bite I'm going to do two things right away. As captain I'll hit the MOB (Man Overboard) button on the GPS. That will mark the spot. Then I'm going to put the boat into a slow turn into the side with the fish. The MOB mark will allow me to return to the exact spot to try to get more bites, and the turn will help keep the rigs from tangling as the angler fights the fish. Always pay attention to the lines and if they cross the crew needs to do the OVER-UNDER dance and get them separated, often switching sides in the process.

When we get the fish up to the boat, we make sure not to reel in too much so that the leader guy has enough room to work with. If you reel in to, far, you risk busting the tip of your rod if the fish suddenly surges or as it's lifted into the boat. The leader person should grab the center of the rig with one hand and lift up, grabbing any lengthy leaders with the other hand, then lifting everything into the boat in one swoop. If you have a fish that is large or one that doesn't look well-hooked, use a net.

If they're hooked well and you're not afraid of breaking them off, grab the center of the frame and lift everything into the boat in one swoop.

Because the fish are of prime concern, we want to unhook them quickly and make a fast decision to tag and release or to keep some.

Once the fish are taken care of, it's time to untangle the rigs, check them over, and get them back in the water to catch again.

Untangling the rigs works best when one person holds the center and another untwists the leader and fixes the baits. Often times the worst of tangles can be undone by simply sliding your fingers down between the leaders and letting the baits unspin themselves.

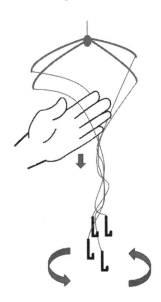

If there isn't an additional person around to hold the center (like when fishing alone), hook an arm of the frame around the reel handle or something else that sticks up so that it stays fixed. Then you can work on the leaders.

It's helpful to have a spare rig or two handy, and if the rigs are too tangled or need repair, you can simply switch them. Then work on the rig that needs attention while you're waiting for your next bite. Maximizing the time the rigs are in the water will maximize your catch.

Before putting an umbrella out, and every time you bring it in, inspect the rig for any issues. If it has leaders, check for nicks and frays. If you find a damaged leader, replace it before it breaks with a fish on it. Whether fishing tubes or shads, check that none of the baits or teasers have slid up or down so that they won't swim correctly. Adjust if necessary.

Certain species of fish such as bass tend to be slower or more opportunistic feeders than others. As a result, you can often catch them below other fish that are blitzing or working on the surface. One day when leaving the harbor we saw a bunch of slicks and birds working. There were a few bluefish busting here and there and a bunch of boats casting top water lures to them – occasionally catching one. Recognizing these good signs, we put a pair of umbrellas out on some wire flat lines. Right away we began catching some keeper-sized stripers that were laying low and picking off the remnants from the bluefish attacks. While everyone else continued to focus on the bluefish (or pass the spot by completely to run to yesterday's hot spot), we trolled the spot for an hour and half and ended up having a nice catch of stripers right out from under everybody.

Mary D'Agostino with a striped bass caught on umbrellas from underneath a school of working bluefish.

Fishing Freshwater Umbrellas

While most umbrella fishing in saltwater is done by trolling, umbrella fishing in freshwater is usually done by casting. Therefore I've devoted this chapter exclusively to freshwater issues. We'll start with an overview of the best tackle to use with CURs and then consider the finer points of fishing them. Dan Vesuvio, Troy Lehew, and Shane Lehew were kind enough to help me out with a lot of the following information. Dan is with Picasso Baits, makers of fine tackle and umbrella rigs. Shane is a bass professional who fishes the FLW Tour (in addition to running Shane's Baits with his father, Troy).

Tackle

There is a consensus among bass pros that if you're going to fish umbrellas, use a rod that's seven to eight feet long to help throw these rigs. A medium-heavy to heavy-weight class is also suggested since these rigs will weigh several ounces. You still want some flexibility in the tip as it helps develop some load when casting, so stay away from broomstick-type models. You also want it to be comfortable while casting, so don't go with one that's too long for you. An exception is if you're finesse casting around docks or structures. Then you might want to go a tad shorter for better control.

Long rods with some flex in the tip are the norm for fishing umbrellas. (Photo Courtesy of FLW/Photographer Jodie White)

A high speed reel with a retrieve ratio of 6.5:1, or thereabouts, is best
for fishing these rigs. While you can fish them on spinning reels, you'll
get better results using bait casting gear.

Initially anglers fished these rigs on a beefy line like a 50 to 65 lb. test
braid, but today freshwater umbrella sharpies are moving to a fluorocarbon line. They prefer fluorocarbon for its ability to sink better, and for
its lower visibility in th water. Shane Lehew, a pro on the FLW tour, goes
with 20-25lb test fluorocarbon to toss his umbrella rigs. He likes the fact
that the fluorocarbon line has some stretch whereas braid does not, and
yet fluorocarbon doesn't stretch as much as monofilament. Unless you're
fishing around heavy cover, you don't need the heavy braid.

For umbrella baits, match the hatch as best you can. If you're seeing
smaller baits in the area, throw a rig with smaller baits. Start with something in the 4 to 5 inch range, and then work smaller if you're not having
success.

Fishing the Rigs:

When on the water, the first priority is finding fish that are susceptible
to the umbrella technique. Study maps of the areas that you'll be fishing, and use your electronics to identify potential hot spots. Your depth

sounder will help locate schooling bait and deeper water humps, ledges, and areas where creek beds or river channels may cross.

Notice this pro angler has his electronics front and center as he's fishing (Photo courtesy of FLW/Photographer Shane Durrance).

Submerged creek beds or river channels, boat lanes and areas around bridges are all prime spots. If there's a bit of current, all the better! Finding suspended bass is ideal for fishing these rigs. Bass will suspend just below a feeding zone and wait for schools of bait to come in. Shad tend to stay away from heavy cover where they can be ambushed and would rather stay in more open areas where they school together. Look again at submerged river beds and travel lanes away from shore where the bait will likely be traveling.

Bridge abutments can be an excellent place to throw umbrellas.
(Photo courtesy of FLW/Photographer Jesse Schultz)

Watch for bird activity as you move about the lake, river, or body of water. When schooling bass feed, they often make baitfish drive to the surface where they also become prey for birds. Birds circling a spot and dipping down to the surface is a tell-tale sign that bait is near the surface.

One of the best things you can learn while fishing umbrellas is to countdown your bait. For a given weight rig (1 oz., 2 oz., 3 oz., etc.), know how fast the rig will sink in feet per second. Once you learn the general sink rates, then you count as your bait hits the water and begins sinking. You'll know how deep you're fishing. This is especially important when targeting suspended fish since you need to be sure you've set your baits at the appropriate level. Find the depth of water at a spot, and then cast to that spot. Allow your rig to sink but start counting as soon as it hits the water. Stop when you feel the rig bounce the bottom. Divide the depth of the water by the time you count and you have your sink rate.

If you cast to an area that's 15 feet deep and it took 10 seconds then you know your rate is 1.5 feet per second. Now, if you are marking fish that are suspended at 9 feet down, you know you want to count to approximately 6 (6 times 1.5 = 9), and then start your retrieve. It sounds basic and you're probably saying "yeah, yeah, yeah, that's obvious," but you'd be amazed by how many anglers don't practice this.

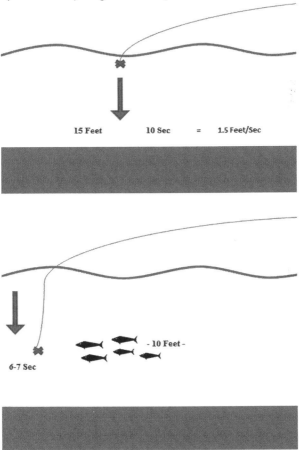

15 Feet   10 Sec   =   1.5 Feet/Sec

- 10 Feet -

6-7 Sec

Learn to count down your baits so that you make sure you're fishing the proper depths.

Even before making a cast, check your rig in the water alongside the boat. Make sure that its fishing properly. If the baits are not running freely, take a few seconds to adjust them until they are. Make sure everything is working exactly the way you want before throwing out to look for a fish. There's no point in sending the rig out if it's not right as you'll only spook the fish.

It pays to experiment with different speed retrieves and occasionally to pause your retrieve. Give an occasional jig or twitch to the rig. Unlike the saltwater versions that have leaders, you can jig a castable umbrella rig because it has no leaders. As with any lure, sometimes the fish want them moving a little faster or a little slower to peak their interest. As the water cools or as you work deeper areas, you want to slow that retrieve down a bit. Fish tend to get more lethargic in cooler water and are not as inclined to chase easily. As water temperature warms or as you work shallower, you may be better off speeding your retrieve up a little. Traditionally umbrellas work better when its cooler (in spring and fall). That said, you can catch all season long with them.

Most professionals I spoke to prefer fishing the umbrella rig in a little bit of wind. If it's windy, you can get away with reeling more consistently. When it's calm you'll want to give the rig a bit of pulse or some erratic movement.

Don't be afraid to change up your bait size. While 5" is generally the largest you'll need in freshwater, if you're not getting bites go ahead and change them up. On some days the fish want something a little smaller or a little larger. Typically when the water is warmer fish strike at larger baits, and when the water is cooler and they are more lethargic, they'll favor the smaller baits.

Sometimes making marks on your baits makes them stand out and gives the fish something to lock in on. This can be done with a marker or paint pen and may be as simple as a black dot. If water visibility is low, it may be a fluorescent, chartreuse or brighter mark.

ENVIRONMENTAL FACTORS ON FISHING FRESHWATER UMBRELLAS		
Water Temperatures	Size of Baits	Retrieve Speed
Warmer	Fish larger baits	Speed up your retrieve.
Cooler	Down size your baits some	Slow your retrieve speed.
Water Clarity	Size of Baits	Bait Color
Clear	Down size your baits some	Use more natural colored baits or clear type baits.
Dirty	Fish larger baits	Use more contrasting and /or brighter colored baits.

The shear design of umbrellas might suggest that you stay away from fishing near cover, but don't hold back. While you do have more hooks that can get caught with these rigs, you can rig them to minimize getting caught on weeds and to reduce snags. Use weedless worm hooks or weedless jig heads. If you need weight, keep some weight in the center bait to help balance the rig. As mentioned earlier, you may want a shorter rod for more finesse casting, but don't be afraid to let them fly towards cover.

If you find yourself fishing cover frequently, it will be worth the investment to purchase a lure retriever that helps with hang ups. A telescoping one fits nicely in a storage hatch or can be latched on deck with your spare rods. Saving just a few lures more than pays for the retriever.

As with saltwater versions, check your baits after you catch a fish, or after you get hung up on something, and every few casts. Make sure the baits and teasers are still fishing correctly. If one is bitten apart or is sliding off, add a little glue or replace it. Keep every component on your rig fishing correctly.

Know your rules

Most states have issued regulations that pertain to the use of umbrellas in freshwater fishing. Some specify the number of hooks allowed, or the size of the hooks allowed. It's smart to know the rules of the game ahead of time since ignorance of the law won't save you from a ticket. This doesn't necessarily mean you can't use your umbrellas in states with rules. It just means that you may have to replace a few of the hook baits with teasers (or remove them) to bring the amount and size of hooks into compliance. You can simply change a couple of the baits via snaps and replace them with a hookless version like a Dummy Head. When removing hook baits, remove the ones towards the front and/or top first. Fish are most likely going to strike from below or behind, so go with the odds in your favor and leave the bottom hooks.

If you're fishing in a tournament, you definitely want to clarify any rules on the use of umbrella rigs. Some tournaments allow them, and others don't. So check prior to fishing.

Tournaments can be fun but know what rigs are legal before you fish them. (Photo Courtesy of FLW/Photographer Curtis Niedermier)

As mentioned before, just because most freshwater umbrella fishing is done by casting, don't overlook this rig's ability to be trolled. If you're just out to have fun and catch a few fish, you may be pleasantly surprised. Who knows, you might start the next trend!

And in closing, I'll leave off with some great advice from Shane Lehew: "If you want to get good at fishing it, don't put it down! Eventually you're going to come across the right fish." It highlights that you need to keep using them in order to get better at fishing them. It also makes the point that not every fish is best caught on an umbrella, but when you find the ones that are, watch out!

Storage Solutions

O ne of the most difficult aspects of fishing with umbrella rigs is how to store them when not in use. Because of their size, their floppy nature, and because they have numerous hooks and often several leaders extending off of them, they like to get caught up with anything and everything.

If you loop a rubber band around all of the hook baits and then put one of the hooks through the eye on the center body, it will help them stay together. While a good rubber band will hold several hook baits together, the leaders still tend to catch on everything. Rubber bands also tend to dry up over time and fall apart, especially on a boat with lots of sun. You can buy UV resistant rubber bands which will help.

Options for storage: Plastic tubes work great for larger rigs. Notice the rectangular bag curling up.

You can also buy plastic tackle storage bags built specifically to hold umbrellas or spreader bars for offshore fishing. The ones made in more of a square shape than a rectangular shape are best to store umbrellas. Nantucket Bags makes a good one. While you can collapse umbrellas into the rectangular ones by squeezing the arms together, they'll tend to want to curl up rather than lie flat.

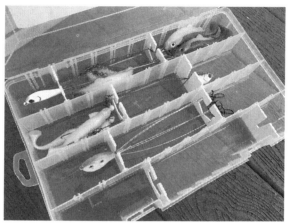

Plastic storage box for CURs

Short sections of 4-6" diameter PVC tubing or pipe also work for storage if your umbrella arms are somewhat flexible. Lighter weight tubes are better as they're easier to handle and carry around. You can find some nice ones online like those made by 9ers Lures of Massachusetts. They're see-through and complete with covers so they stay contained and you're able to see what rig is inside. Their only drawback is that because they are round they love to roll around in a boat if you don't have a way to effectively store the tubes.

A homemade alternative is to use the plastic zipper bags that come with pillows or blankets. The plastic is usually strong enough to prevent easy hooking and fold up when not in use. While they won't hold up to years of abuse, they can usually get you through a season or two.

Storage is a little easier for freshwater equipment. You can simply buy a clear Plano storage box (Model 3708). It holds up to four of these rigs. The arms will easily squeeze together, and the rigs slide neatly into storage spaces that have grooved slots to hold the head and arms. It's easy to get the rigs in and out of them, and you can carry several together.

Small tubes will also work. Squeeze the rig's arms together and slide them into the tubes. You'll need a small bag or box of some type to keep the tubes together.

There are other products on the market that do the job - various forms of wraps or boxes. Straight plastic boxes will work as well as long as you have something like a ring or rubber band to keep the arms together.

I've also seen guys use large, empty plastic juice bottles (the kind with the wide mouths) for storage. They cut the bottoms off and slide them over a rig that's slightly squeezed together. Some even store them this way with the rig still on the rod. It's a great way to go if you transport your rods with the rigs on and want to avoid snagging passengers.

While running to the grounds or from spot to spot, make sure that the rig either sits flat on the deck, that the frame itself is hooked against the reel handle, or that the hooks are hooked to the reel. You don't want them swinging around to catch and and hurt someone. If you thought one hook hurt – try four or five!

Note that all four hooks are secured to the reel for safety.

Other Helpful Aspects

The following is related material that will help with umbrella rig fishing and rigging.

Improved Clinch Knot

Learn this knot if you don't already know it. The majority of time I use an improved clinch knot. It's very strong and is super easy to tie. Among other uses, I use this knot for attaching the snap swivel to my line, and for attaching arm leaders to their swivels on both the arm and the hook. You can use any knot you like, but this one has worked extremely well for me.

- To tie it, begin by running the end of the line through the swivel eye (or whatever you are connecting to) and pull it through about 6 or 7 inches.
- Twist the tag end around the main line about 7 or 8 times, working away from the swivel.
- Bring the tag end back through the loop that is created just above the swivel.
- Now bring the tag end through the loop formed by bringing the tag end down to that first loop.
- Moisten the knot with a little saliva so that it will slide easily and, while holding the tag end just so that it doesn't pull out, pull on the main line and swivel in opposite directions so that the knot is pulled tight.
- Clip your tag end off close to the knot.

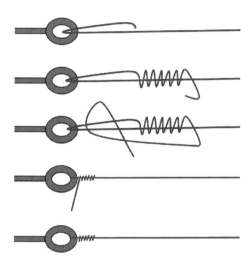

Lead Core Setup

When setting up my rigs with lead core line for trolling, I'll use the following configuration:

- a six to eight foot fluorocarbon leader
- a 300 foot section of lead core line. (I usually use Tuf-Line MicroLead #27 lb. test. It's thinner than most lead core lines so you can get more on the reel, it has less drag in the water, and it seems to get deeper.)
- Dacron or mono backing to fill the remainder of the spool

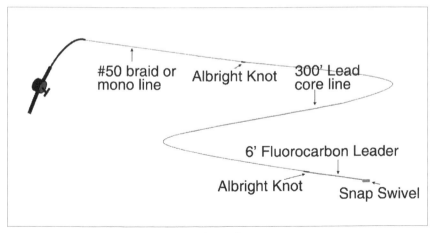

Lead Core Setup

So that clients know exactly where to set the lines without having to count color sections (and so I can easily double check them), I'll mark certain lengths with a few half hitches of dental floss. Usually I'll put one mark at 100 feet, two marks at 150 feet, and three marks at 200 feet.

Lead Core – Albright Knot

When fishing with lead core line, it's good to have a solid knot for connecting a fluorocarbon or mono leader. When I rig my lead core setups, I'll use an Albright knot to make this connection. It takes a little practice to get it down. It also helps to have a strong paper clip, tooth pick, or thin nail to help give the lead core some support when you're wrapping the leader around it.

Here are the basics:

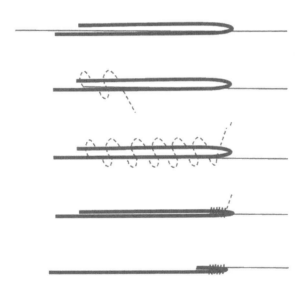

The Albright Knot

- Fold over the end of the lead core line about three inches.
- Hold a straightened out paper clip (or other firm slim object) up tight next to the end of the lead core line.
- Begin by bringing the tag end of the leader through the

loop created in the lead core line and bring it through about 8 to 10 inches.

- Starting about three quarters to an inch from the end of the doubled over lead core (loop), start wrapping the leader around the lead core and paper clip just tight enough that each wrap lies nicely next to the next one – working back towards the end of the lead core/loop.
- Once you've wrapped it about 8-10 times you should be nearing the end of the lead core and the tag end of the leader can go back through the loop at the end of the lead core. Pull it through so that there's no slack left.
- Holding the tag end just enough so that it doesn't pull back through, pull the lead core main line and the main leader line in opposite directions to snug the knot up.
- Trim the tag end of the leader close to the knot and trim the lead core about a ¼" from the knot. A couple of wraps of floss around the tag end of the lead core will keep it neat but is not needed.

Wire Line Setup

To me, for fishing in the northeast, the premiere way to troll an umbrella rig is with wire line or lead-core. Wire takes some practice to fish with and it requires specific methods to rig it effectively. For that, I've included some diagrams, photos, and steps to help you rig up your wire line.

These are all methods we use aboard my boat the *SHEARWATER*. If you're not up to going through these steps, most tackle shops worth their money can set this up for you. You can also do something different that works for you.

My wire outfits are on the lighter side. Starting from the rod tip end, they consist of the following:

- A 10' fluorocarbon or mono leader.
- 100' of 0.020 Inconel wire
- 3' section of black #200 or #130 lb. test Dacron–"B"
- 50' of #30lb test Inconel wire
- 3' section of #135 lb. test Yellow Dacron -"Y"

- 50' of #30lb test Inconel wire
- 3' Section of #135 lb. test Orange Dacron -"O"
- 50' of #30lb test Inconel wire
- 3'Section of #200 or #130 lb. test black Dacron - "B"
- 50' of #30lb test Inconel wire
- Either a braid or mono line backing to fill out spool

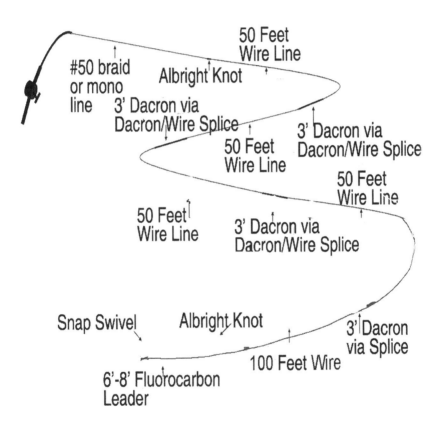

Wire Line Setup

Using the wire line setup, I can measure how much line I have out by observing which Dacron section is showing – (100'/150'/200'/250') or by seeing I'm all the way to the backing (300'). I like the black-yellow-orange-black (B-Y-O-B) color schema. It's an easy sequence to remember: 'Buy-Your-Own-Boat' (or if you're having a bad day, 'Bring-Your-Own-Bass').

Fishing to one of these Dacron intervals at the rod tip helps alleviate stress on the wire at the rod tip while trolling. Dacron is more forgiving while the tip works back and forth due to changes in boat speed, movement from waves, and bounces from fish, weeds, or the bottom.

You can substitute monofilament sections for each Dacron section. If you go this route, you'll need to use Albright knots instead of the Dacron splices. The Dacron splice is a little slimmer than the knots so it slides through the guides better, but either will work.

Some guys mark their wire line with a swivel, colored plastic tape, or with small sections of telephone wire. I don't like using swivels because of the difficulty they can have going cleanly through guides. A good plastic tape will work but will eventually find a way to slide (losing its distance spot) or it may fall off at some point. Pieces of colored phone wire wrapped on at measured intervals also works. It lasts better than the tape and goes through guides easier than swivels. None of these alternatives however solve the issue of wear on the wire from the rod tip.

Wire Line Knots – Albright

This is almost identical to the lead core Albright above, but when you've finished tying the leader in, I melt the mono tag end (being careful not to melt the leader itself or the knot). I also finish the tag end of the wire with a few barrel wraps to prevent any slippage.

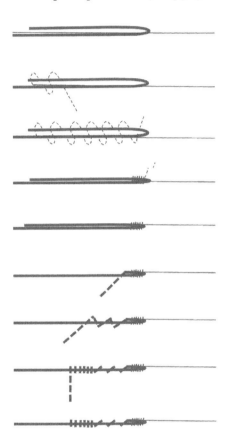

Wire Line Knots – Dacron Splice

In order to create the Dacron marking/working sections in my wire setups, here are the steps to splice the Dacron and wire:

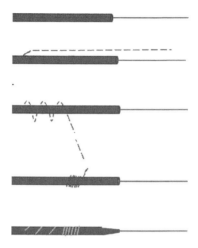

- Take the end of the wire and make sure that the last 6" is nice and straight
- Insert the wire end into the hollow center of the Dacron and slowly push it up in.
- Using your other hand or fingers, help guide the Dacron over the wire so it slides at least 2" to 3" up into the Dacron. Then poke it through the Dacron casing so that it comes out the side.
- Pull about 4 or 5" of wire out the side and create a sharp 180 degree bend in it. You may need to squeeze it together slightly to make it fairly compressed.
- Pull the wire from the standing end back towards where it comes out of the Dacron so that the bend rests where it comes out of the Dacron casing.
- Using a pair of pliers, hold it tight, and coming down about a half inch from where it exits the casing, slowly wind it around the Dacron (with the wire through it) for about three quarters of an inch (maybe 5 or 6 wraps).
- Then do 5 or 6 tight barrel wraps to lock it up, breaking off the wire tag end slowly.

Next, take a match (or a lighter) and slightly melt the tip end where the Dacron meets the wire. As it starts melting, take a damp rag and run it over the melting Dacron to extinguish it and smooth it tight to the wire. It will form a sort of taper. You could apply a touch of Zap-a-gap or super glue if you want to insure against unraveling while it goes through the guides. I usually don't use the glue as I re-do my connections periodically anyway, so I just leave mine as is after melting.

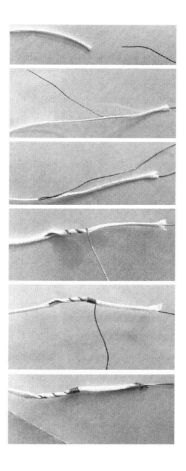

Dying Latex Tubing

If you want to try your hand at dying some latex tubing to create your own colors here are the basic steps:

- Make sure your working in an area that is not going to get you in trouble if a little spills or splashes.
- Take a large can (old coffee can) or bucket that is capable of holding boiling water.
- Bring some water to boil and pour into a can or bucket.
- Take a packet of RIT or Tintex dye and stir it into the water so that it's mixed thoroughly and evenly.
- Add your latex tubing, and let it soak for about 5 minutes.
- Remove the tubing carefully, and place it on something disposable (like cardboard) and allow it to cool off.
- Once it's cooled off you should rinse it well to remove any residue and help prevent bleeding.

I've heard some say that they will still get some dye bleeding off onto their cabin cushions or seats when the rigs are stored so be warned. Others swear that if you do it right and rinse it thoroughly, you won't get any bleeding.

If you're going to be doing multiple sections of tubing, be sure to keep the dye water heated, It needs to be warm to effectively color the tubing.

I usually buy my tubing already colored. It's simply easier and there isn't a significant difference in cost. But if you want a custom color, a two-tone pattern (like heads orange and tails green), or some other unique combination, then this is your way to go.

Creating a Safety Line for your Trolling Rod

When trolling, especially with rod riggers where the rod is out to the side, it's important to use a safety line on the rod and reel. If it does go over the side, you can retrieve it. This is a lesson from experience. I use either a 3 strand nylon or a braid rope section. The steps to create one are as follows:

- First, locate where on your boat you're going to secure the end to – whether it's a cleat, a seat pedestal, rail, or whatever. It should be something secure.
- Using a length of the rope to measure, loop it around the point you will secure it on, and then string it over to where your reel will be while in trolling position. Make sure to allow for the slack or drooping you want. I leave enough so that the line will lay flat on the deck and not trip anyone. I also add a little extra so that it can reach the opposite side of my small skiff. This way, if I have two anglers that need to swap positions quickly, they can.
- Once you have it measured, add enough length to both ends for whatever knot or splice you're going to do. Now you have your overall length.
- I usually do a spliced loop in one end (for attaching it securely to the boat), and a stainless or brass lobster clasp (or spring clip) on the other for attaching it directly to the reel. I prefer to clip mine to a safety loop on the back of the reel clamp so that it doesn't interfere with reeling when we get a fish on. If you don't have a safety loop on the reel clamp, then you can go to the eyes on the front of the reel (if it has them) or use a tight wrap around the rod grip in front of the reel if you have nothing else to clip it to.

Line Winding

Because wire kinks easily, it's best to have two people when putting it on your reels. One person holds the spool while the other reels it on. If you don't have a second person available, use some type of line winder. Being able to spread out (for example in the backyard) is helpful too. Borrowing a trick I learned years ago from Capt. Anderson, I made two large wooden spools to measure out lines and to reverse them if needed. I measure the circumference of the spool to get what one turn measures in length. If the circumference comes out to a foot and a half then I know that a 50 foot section takes 33 and half turns.

Large spools that you can turn by hand assist greatly in measuring, marking, and reversing lines.

Twists, Issues, and Fish On

Throughout the years I have experimented with the setup of umbrellas in different situations. Using one that had an arm broken off (so it was reduced to three arms), I cut the clip off the end and loaded on a few egg sinkers to the center arm, leaving the tube teasers on the other two. I then attached two leaders to the other two arms with fluke rigs and used this setup to slow troll the bottom whenever our fluke drift died out.

The arm with the sinkers bounced off the bottom and kept the rig in the fluke's strike zone. While we didn't crush them, we did manage to catch several fluke at a slack period when we were otherwise not catching at all.

Fluke will hit umbrella rigs as well.

I've also tried rigging one up with rubber squids for trolling up some fluke. To do this, you usually have to add some weights to any of the squids rigged on the leaders. Doing so will prevent them from floating up higher than the rig and then tangling.

I've had some success with fluke and an occasional bluefish, but I don't think my rigs had quite enough action to them. The next time I try using squids, I'll add some type of swimming head to the squid first, perhaps something that puts a wiggle in their step (or swim).

I tried versions rigged with metal spoons that ended up working on bluefish, but I didn't see much success with other fish. If using spoons try using one that has a wobble so it swims nicely and sends off some vibration. They may work better if the water is dirty, for example after a storm.

In the early spring when fishing in local salt ponds or rivers, I'll sometimes fish a version rigged with Cocahoe Minnows. Their paddle tail gives them a great swimming action, and the small slender bait style works well.

A happy angler with a trio of school
stripers caught in a salt pond on
an umbrella of cocahoe minnows

My point is: keep experimenting. You never know when you might be onto the next big phase of this rig. When trying a new bait, I like to experiment in a two prong approach. I like to try the experimental version during both a good bite and a slow bite. While the slow periods seem like the best times to experiment because you're not missing much and you never know when the fish just want something different, it's also difficult to tell what's a pattern or an isolated instance when the bites are few and far in between. Was it a pattern or was it just dumb luck? So I experiment during periods of a good bite - to see if there's a decline in the bites with the new version. Then I know my idea was not quite as good as I thought.

While this lure continues to be one of the hottest fishing items, it's use is not without debate - for both saltwater and freshwater fishing. Certain tournaments, the IGFA and many states, have made some rules relative to the use of the umbrella rig. In some cases, it's banned completely.

Tournaments

Some professional freshwater tournaments ban the use of the umbrella rig, even if the number of hooks is reduced. Others do not. The FLW allows the rigs in the TBF/FLW High School Fishing, FLW College Fishing , FLW Bass Fishing League (BFL) Series ,Costa FLW Series. The Walmart FLW Tour (at time of this writing) does not allow it.

Some that do allow it stipulate however that: *"Alabama rigs and similar umbrella-type rigs are limited to a maximum of five wires with a maximum of five spinners, five lures and three hooks (single or treble) unless state regulations are more restrictive, in which case state regulations prevail."*

These restrictions do not apply to all tournaments, but it's best to check ahead and see if the umbrella rig can be part of your game plan.

If you're going to fish tournaments make sure to know the rules regarding the use of umbrellas beforehand. (Photo Courtesy of FLW/Photographer Jodie White).

IGFA

The International Game Fish Association is a well-known and well respected organization and is the keeper of world-wide sport fishing records. For anglers interested in pursuing potential world record catches, the IGFA has a very detailed rule book that outlines the requirements are for each type of fishing. It covers the rules relative to the fishing rods that can be used, the reels, line requirements, leader regulations, bait/lure criteria, and angling approaches. Because this book deals solely with the use of umbrella rigs, I felt that it would be important to provide readers with the IGFA rules (as of time of printing of course) that pertain to the use of umbrella rigs.

Simply put, in submissions for potential records the IGFA does not allow the use of umbrella rigs (or spreader bars, etc.) when they are attached directly to your line. The view is that the rig may impede the fish's ability to fight, and it is therefore deemed unfair. However, you can still use one as long as your line is connected to the umbrella through a release device that allows the line to break free of the rig once you hook up. In this case, the umbrella rig essentially becomes a teaser.

While I have not personally seen anyone use this approach, if one were serious about going after a world record, I suspect that it could be done and would be an effective way to get bites. If you desired to try this method, you should attach the line (not the leader) to the umbrella frame with either a rubber band or some sort of a release clip. That said, if you're looking to catch a world record, it would be prudent to read up on current rules to clarify any questions you have before landing a fish for the scales.

State Laws

Most states have detailed regulations for the use of umbrellas and/or allowable tackle in freshwater bodies of water. Some are simple restrictions on the size or the number of hooks, while others restrictions are more encompassing. The laws do not necessarily mean that the use of umbrellas are illegal, but usually limit how many baits with hooks that you can have. You can always replace hook baits with teasers and or dummy heads so your rig meets local regulations. What's important is that you know the rules before fishing, so check with the local fish and wildlife office.

Don't let these stipulations change your mind about this rig. Some of the same anglers that argue against its use in bass tournaments, say that it provides "an unfair advantage." These same advocates often accept other methods of fishing that can be even more damaging to the fishery or are "less competitive" when it comes to the sport. The tactic to find freshwater bass on their beds and catch them is well known and a highly practiced method. The fish are in the process of reproducing, and they are protecting their nests. The reason they strike at baits at this time isn't because they're lured by the bait itself, but rather it is a defensive measure to protect their nest. We know these fish will be aggressive in protecting their beds and thus they are more readily catchable.

The IGFA's ban of umbrella rigs in tournaments stems from two specific points: (1) they use multiple hooks, and (2), the frame itself is deemed to hamper the fish's ability to fight. For these reasons the ban also includes spreader bars and often the daisy chains used offshore when trolling.

Wire line fishing is one of the most commonly used methods of trolling inshore gamefish in the northeast but the very use of wire line is banned by the IGFA. If you want to have fun fishing and you want to have the best chance for some action, then use the best available rig options: wire lines and umbrella rigs. If you want to go after world record catches, you will need to review the full set of applicable IGFA rules in detail. Make sure all aspects of your setup and bait meet their requirements. Both kinds of fishing have their place and should be respected.

My Views, and My Views Only

Obviously I look favorably on umbrella rigs and believe they are a great tool for catching fish. They aren't for everyone or for every occasion. There are times when other baits or lures are better choices. I don't believe using an umbrella rig makes it any less or any more competitive than other options. The intent isn't to use the rig as a means to snag fish - if that were the case it would be better to simply use oversized treble hooks. Instead the intent is to entice the fish to biting them as bait.

Not everyone will prefer the same method of fishing. That's why we have fly fisherman, surf fisherman, offshore fisherman, flats fisherman, your trout fisherman, and bass fisherman. We have anglers using kites, boats using green sticks, and boats fishing with downriggers. Different methods work for different fish in different situations. Some like using light tackle, and some prefer a quicker fight to release fish quicker. It's a matter of personal preference.

Some claim that fish finders, side scanning sonar, color selectors, Global Positioning Systems (GPS), and even plastic worms are unfair. There are many styles and purposes to this sport. Each will have different appeals and different approaches, and we should respect that.

It's worth remembering that using an umbrella rig doesn't guarantee a catch. You still have to find the fish, get the rigs in front of them, and entice them to strike. That's the same as with any other bait or lure.

You also still have the same bag limit, so you're not keeping any more fish with umbrellas than with any other method of fishing.

A full bag of bluefish

Some people have expressed concerns that the umbrella rig's hooks could snag the fish's body when they are already hooked through the mouth. I have not seen this often fishing saltwater, but I have seen it on occasion fishing in freshwater with CURs. I believe it's more common when you have hooks connected directly to the wire frames instead of on leaders where they are much more ridged and prone to grab rather than bounce off. I've also seen fish hooked this way when fishing larger casting plugs where the fish has one hook in the mouth and the other hook snags the body.

We've covered a lot of aspects of fishing the umbrella rigs here and hopefully it has given you some new insights into fishing this rig. While the rig may not be for everybody, there's no question that it's very productive.

Keep in mind that the methods mentioned here to rig it are not all-inclusive. I don't mean to suggest that the ways to rig that I've outlined are the only ones that work. I've discussed methods that work for me and other professional anglers, but in fact, the rigging possibilities are endless. All you need to do is to find what works for you on the body of water that you fish. Perhaps you'll discover the next hot way to fish this rig.

So what is the answer to what's the most fish I've caught at one time on the umbrella? It happens to be 5 bluefish on a 4 hook rig. One of the fish must have been striking at the teasers and it actually got lassoed by one of the arm leaders. The pull of the fish on the leader that lassoed it must have kept it so tight that he couldn't escape. Now before you go saying "see – umbrellas are unfair", it's important to note that I've also caught fish this way while bait fishing with one hook. The fish (a school tuna) must have missed the bait, and the hook flipped around and caught the line further up, lassoing the fish in the process. So it can happen with either rig.

Conservation

Because the umbrella rig is a very effective rig, it therefore imposes an even stronger need for a commitment to conservation. Aboard my boat the *SHEARWATER,* we encourage tag and release of all fish that are not going to be readily eaten. We tag a significant number of fish each year for the American Littoral Society. Tagging helps them study the way fish migrate and grow while in their natural environment (as opposed to in a tank somewhere).

While Fish and Wildlife departments set regulations to try to maintain healthy stock levels and to prevent overfishing, as users of the resource we need to hold ourselves to even stronger standards and be committed to keeping the resource strong. We can't rely on state or federal authorities to be the sole regulator. We need to regulate ourselves. This doesn't mean we can't keep a few fish for the grill. It only means that we shouldn't take more than we can use. Keep conserving and keep fishing.

Eric Therrien and Mary D'Agostino with a school-sized striped bass caught on an umbrella rig and then tagged and released for the American Littoral Society

I'm hoping that you've enjoyed this book, and that you picked up a few things about fishing these great rigs. Now it's time to get out on the water and send them an umbrella.

I hope you have many tight lines ahead.

Capt. Steve Tombs

GLOSSARY

Alabama Rig: This was the name given to the first castable umbrella rig invented by Andy Poss. It's really a brand but is often used interchangeably by fisherman to refer to the castable umbrella rig (CUR).

Bait Keeper: (Similar to a centering pin or bait spring) A small, screw-like wire with a loop on one end and a screw on the other end. The screw end is inserted into a plastic bait so that it can be attached via the loop.

Bait Spring: (Similar to a centering pin or bait keeper) A small, screw like, wire that has a loop on one end and a screw on the other end. The screw end is inserted into a plastic bait so that it can be attached via the loop.

Barrel Swivel: A small connecting device used on fishing lines to prevent the line from twisting. It has a round eye on each end and sort of a barrel-shaped body in the middle. Each end spins within itself to absorb any twist.

Bead Chain Swivel: A swivel that is made of a length of bead chain with an eye on each end.

Blades: Willow leaf or other metal spinners similar to those used on spinner bait rigs. They are sometimes used on umbrella rigs to create flash and vibration.

Castable Umbrella Rig (CUR): A smaller version of the umbrella rig that does not have any leaders so that it's able to be casted without tanging up.

Centering Pins: (Similar to a bait keeper) A small, screw like, wire that has a loop on one end and a screw (with a pin in the center) on the other end. The screw end is inserted into a plastic bait so that it can be attached via the loop.

Downrigger: A device that has a heavy arm, a large spool with cable, and a heavy 5-10 lb weight on the end that can be used to bring your line to deeper depths while trolling. The fishing line is attached via a release clip that pops free when a fish strikes.

Dredge: Is a metal or wire type frame that is used to hold many baits. Sometimes several frames are connected together to simulate a large bait school. Typically, the term is used more often today to describe offshore teasers (no hooks) that are used to draw pelagic fish such as marlin in closer to then try and hook them with another bait. Typically dredges are heavy and trolled off outriggers, downriggers, cleats, or heavy duty rods.

Dummy head: A jig that does not have a hook, but rather has a screw or clip used to attach a plastic bait for the purpose of being a teaser or attractant.

Duolock Snap: A type of clip used in fishing to connect two objects, like a swivel and a lure. Its interlocking design allows each end to act as a separate clip.

Flat Line: A rod that is fished directly to the lure and not run through any other device (such as an outrigger, downrigger, etc.).

Frame: The wire and center component of the umbrella rig which essentially holds the rig together.

Hook Bait: A bait or lure that contains the fishing hook meant to catch a fish on.

Leader: A length of line, wire, or cable that is used in between the bait or lure and the fishing line to help prevent loss due to chafing or bite offs. A leader can also be used to hold onto to assist in landing a fish.

Rig: A fishing setup consisting of one or several lures and/or teasers

Rod riggers: A type of fishing rod holder that holds the tip of the rod out to the side of the boat instead of up high. This keeps the line and rod lower to the water and further away from the boat.

Safety Line: A piece of rope or line fastened at one end to the boat while the other end attaches to the reel. If a rod were to fall overboard, pulling the safety line it's attached to helps retrieve it.

Snap Swivel: A connecting device used on fishing lines to both prevent the line from twisting and to be able to connect an object via a clip that locks shut. A snap swivel makes it unnecessary to tie a knot each time.

Split Ring: A circular metal connector used in fishing to attach two things together. You attach items by splitting opening the metal wires and sliding the object on, working it around until it finds its way into the center of the ring

Spreader: Is a wire, metal, or plastic object that is used to spread multiple baits and keep them apart from one another.

Swim Bait: An artificial lure that generates a swimming action when it's retrieved.

Swivel: A small connecting device used on fishing lines to prevent the line from twisting. Each end spins within itself to absorb any twist.

Tag and Release: The process of inserting a metal or plastic identifier (tag) into a fish you catch and then releasing it alive so that its growth and migrations can be studied.

Teaser: An object that is attached to a fishing rig that resembles a bait or lure but does not have a hook. It's used exclusively as an attractor

Trolling Sinker: Usually a cigar, torpedo, or oblong shaped weight that has an eye or snap on each end and can be rigged in-line with your lure for trolling. It's used to gain depth while trolling.

Tube(s): These types of lures are made from some type of tubing or hose such as Latex, vinyl, or plastic. They usually cover a bent style hook that helps them spin in the water.

Umbrella Rig: A multiple lure fishing rig that, through a combination of teasers and hook baits, simulates a school of bait rather than a single bait.

Frames Information & Contacts

Try your local tackle shop, but if you don't find what you need, here are some companies you can turn to:

Picasso Lures, LLC
6222 Tanoma Road
Indiana, PA 15701
Tel: 724-313-8014
www.PicassoOutdoors.com

Shane's Baits
7938 Unity Church Road
Denver, NC 28037
Tel: 704-966-4200
shanesbaits@gmail.com
www.Shanesbaits.com

Osprey Custom Tackle, LLC
9 West Road
Niantic, CT 06357
860-739-4129

9er's Lures
79 Middleboro Ave
Taunton, MA 02780
(508) 822-9650
www.9erslures.com

SUGGESTED READING

Anderson, Capt. Al. *Island Stripers: A Fisherman's Guide to Block Island Bass*. Capt. Al Anderson. Pp 131-136. 2012.

Anderson, Capt. Al. *Over-Winter Striper Secrets*. Capt. Al Anderson. Pp 73-79. 2009

Anderson, Capt. Al. '*Ways with Wire*'. *The Fisherman* magazine, New England Edition. Volume 18, Number 28. Pp 22-23 1991

Anderson, Capt. Al. '*Take a Bead on Stripers: The Ultimate Umbrella*'. *The Fisherman* magazine, New England Edition. Volume 28, Issue 21. Pp 4-5. 5/24/2001

Anderson, Capt. Al. '*Umbrella Rig How-to: Talking about Trailers*'. *The Fisherman* magazine, New England Edition. Pp 18-19. 10/8/1998

Barret, Pete. *Trolling for Striped Bass and Bluefish*. Pete Barret. Pp 48-51. 2007.

Barrett, Pete. '*Umbrella Rig Choices*'. *The Fisherman* magazine, New England Edition. Volume 42.p 58 10/2015

Caolo, Alan. *Fly Fisherman's Guide to Atlantic Baitfish & Other food Sources*. Alan Caolo. 1995

Coleman, Tim. *To Catch a Bass*. MT Publications. Pp 147-153. 1992.

Larsen, Larry. *An Anglers Guide to Bass Patterns*. Larry Larsen. 1990.

Larsen, Larry, *Bass Fishing Facts: An Angler's Guide to Bass Lifestyles and Behavior*. Larry Larsen. Pp 31-60. 1989.

Larsen, Larry. *Follow the Forage for Better Bass Angling: Bass Anglers Guide to Understanding Feeding Activity and Improving Your Catch.* Larry Larsen. 1984

Mermon, Dick. *'Marking Wire Line'. The Fisherman* magazine, New England Edition. Volume 19, Number 16. Pp 22-23 1992

Merrill, Jeff. *'Fisherman's Workbench: Rubber Shad Umbrella Rigs'. The Fisherman* magazine, New England Edition. Pp16-19. 1/4/2001

Ross, David A. *The Fisherman's Ocean: How Marine Science Can Help You Catch More Fish.* David A Ross. 2000.

Schultz, Ken. *Ken Schultz's Fishing Encyclopedia: Worldwide Angling Guide.* IDG Books Worldwide, Inc. pp1816-1817. 2000.

Schultz, Ken. *The Art of Trolling.* Ken Schultz. Pp35-70 .1987.

Sosin, Mark and Clark, James. *Through the Fishes Eye: An Anglers Guide to Gamefish Behavior.* Mark Sosin and James Clark. 1973

About the Author

Captain Steve Tombs

Captain Stephen worked his way through college by taking jobs on local charter fishing boats. Though he earned a degree in Applied Mathematics, what he retained most from his early years is a passion for fishing.

He went on to earn a Masters license from the U.S. Coast Guard, and to run charters on a part time basis. He's a strong believer in "Catch & Release" and frequently tags the fish he catches for the American Littoral Society.

Stephen has over 35 years of experience fishing saltwater. Over the years he's been fortunate enough to have worked with some excellent captains who shared their wealth of knowledge with him. In turn, Steve enjoys passing on his own fishing expertise, and he has done so since the 1980's, publishing tips and his experiences in numerous articles in local fishing magazines.

As Stephen's first book, Catching with Umbrealls gets him deeper into the subject of fishing these rigs more effectively.

Stephen migrated from western Massachusetts to Rhode Island in the 1980's to be near the ocean and lives in Narragansett RI today with his children.

124

Made in the USA
Charleston, SC
03 November 2016